About the Round Table

About the Round Table

THE METROPOLITAN MUSEUM OF ART

ABOUT THE ROUND TABLE
KING ARTHUR IN ART AND LITERATURE

By MARGARET R. SCHERER

NEW YORK, 1945

ARNO PRESS

1974

The author's thanks are due to Laura Hibbard Loomis and Roger Sherman Loomis for their advice and guidance, and to the Modern Language Association of America for permission to use the material appearing in "Arthurian Legends in Medieval Art" by Mr. and Mrs. Loomis.

Thanks are also extended to the Frick Art Reference Library, the Pierpont Morgan Library, and the Fogg Museum of Art for generous assistance in research.

Reprinted by permission of the Metropolitan Museum of Art

LC #76-168428
ISBN 0-405-02266-2

Manufactured in the United States of America

INTRODUCTION: THE GROWTH OF THE ARTHURIAN LEGENDS

The legends of Arthur and his knights are among those great stories of the world which have been told and re-told through centuries, changing their form with successive periods. They are rich in characters and situations of wide human appeal and in the elements of heroic idealism and romantic love which refresh the mind in times when men feel a need for heroes and lovers.

This book presents briefly, in picture and in story, some of the most outstanding tales as they were known in the Middle Ages and as they were revived in the nineteenth century, and suggests the social backgrounds which led to different treatments of the legends in different periods. Some narratives have been taken from French and German romances, but Sir Thomas Malory's fifteenth-century English masterpiece, the *Morte d'Arthur*, has been followed whenever possible, for with his book the international story of this British hero became one of the glories of English literature.

The story of Arthur began more than fourteen centuries ago, but its record in literature and art is not quite so long. The historic Arthur lived about A.D. 500. He was probably a battle leader of the Britons against the Anglo-Saxons who invaded Britain after the Romans had withdrawn. His deeds left such a lasting impression upon his fellow countrymen that, after the Celtic Britons had been absorbed by the invaders or driven into Wales and Cornwall or across the Channel into Brittany, the legend grew up that he was not dead but recovering from his wounds in the fairy island of Avalon and would come again to help his country. In the fanciful tales told among the Welsh and Cornish and their kin, the Bretons of Brittany, Arthur was said to be the king of a band of warriors who could perform all kinds of supernatural feats; he himself had magical powers and possessions

and was an invincible giant killer. But the first written record of Arthur, which is found in the Latin chronicle of the Welshman Nennius, dating about 826, does not call him a king. Nennius called Arthur *dux bellorum*— "leader of battles"—and said that he fought beside the kings of the Britons against the Saxon invaders. His real position may have been like that of the Roman Count of Britain, who had general charge of all military forces in the country.

When the Normans conquered Britain in 1066, the legend of Arthur was already familiar in Normandy as well as in Britain. The Celtic national chieftain was a satisfactory hero to both the Norman conquerors and the vanquished Anglo-Saxons, for he belonged to neither side. Both could appreciate the comment on Arthur made by William of Malmesbury, an English monk, in a Latin chronicle about 1125: "He is the Arthur about whom the Britons [Bretons] rave in empty words, but who, in truth, is worthy to be the subject, not of deceitful tales and dreams, but of true history; for he was long the prop of his tottering fatherland, and spurred the broken spirits of his countrymen on to war."

It was a chronicler of Norman England who first gave literary form to the mass of Arthurian legends and created the heroic figure of Arthur as a great warrior and king. About 1136 this chronicler, Geoffrey of Monmouth, described Arthur's deeds at length in his Latin

---

ABOVE: *The heraldic arms of Sir Lancelot, King Arthur, and Sir Galahad, from The Names, Arms, and Blazons of the Knights of the Round Table. French manuscript, about 1500. In the Pierpont Morgan Library, New York, M16, fols. 26, 4, 23. Slightly enlarged*

Arthur and the Giant of Mont-St.-Michel. Manuscript illumination, Flemish, late XII century, from a copy of Geoffrey of Monmouth's History. In the Douai Library, MS 880, fol. 66

History of the Kings of Britain, which traced the British kings back to Brutus the Trojan, great-grandson of Aeneas. This work was indeed far from the "true history" which William of Malmesbury had desired. Geoffrey told the stories of Arthur as a giant killer and the legend of his departure "unto the island of Avalon for the healing of his wounds." He also described the British leader as a conqueror of most of Europe, who almost became emperor of Rome itself. The pen drawing above, of Arthur killing the Giant of Mont-St.-Michel, perhaps the oldest manuscript picture of the king in existence, comes from a copy of Geoffrey's *History*.

The next chronicler gave Arthur a background and character patterned after the courtly fashion of his own day, when Henry II was king of England and Eleanor of Aquitaine his queen. This chronicler was Wace, a Norman living in England, who wrote, about 1155, a French chronicle in verse, based on Geoffrey's *History* but amplified to suit court tastes. Wace described Arthur as "one of Love's lovers; a lover also of glory; and his famous deeds are right fit to be kept in remembrance. He ordained the courtesies of courts, and observed high state in a very splendid fashion." Wace is the first to mention Arthur's famous Round Table. He speaks in more detail than Geoffrey of the belief in the king's return and says that Arthur was "awaited of the Britons [Bretons]; for as they say and deem he will return from whence he went and live again." But he also remarked:

"Men have ever doubted, and—as I am persuaded—will always doubt whether he liveth or is dead." Wace's critical judgment of the legend might be that of today: "Not all lies, nor all true, all foolishness, nor all sense; so much have the storytellers told, and so much have the makers of fables fabled . . . that they have made all seem fable."

Another chronicler, Layamon, a priest of Worcestershire, told Arthur's story for the first time in English between 1175 and 1205. Although by this time French poets had composed romances concerning Arthur's court, Layamon kept the form of a poetic chronicle of British kings. In language, verse form, and content he emphasized the English rather than the Norman culture of England. Anglo-Saxon and Celtic cultures are blended to make Arthur a national, English hero, who rallies his men against the Saxons, crying: "See ye not, my Britons, here beside us, our full foes? Christ destroy them!" Layamon was much more definite than Wace about Arthur's return, making the king say: "I will fare to Avalun, to the fairest of all maidens, to Argante the queen, an elf most fair, and she shall make my wounds all sound; make me all whole with healing draughts. And afterwards I will come again to my kingdom, and dwell with the Britons with mickle joy." The sceptical Wace, writing for the French-speaking court, made Merlin prophesy of Arthur "that his end should be hidden in doubtfulness." Layamon presented a more hopeful view to his English audience. According to him, Merlin, whose "sayings were sooth," said "that an Arthur should yet come to help the English."

The Welsh descendants of the Celtic Britons clung stubbornly to this prophecy of Merlin's, claiming that the king would return to lead them in their rebellions against the Plantagenet kings of England. A discovery which the English monks of Glastonbury announced in 1191 was probably aimed at disproving this belief. The monks had found, they said, two bodies with an inscription identifying them as those of Arthur and his queen, Guenevere, and had buried them with honor at the abbey. But in spite of this discovery legend continued to say that Arthur lived in Avalon.

Arthur and his knights became heroes of chivalric romance in the second half of the twelfth century. In this half century French poets on the Continent and in Norman England gave literary form to almost all the well-known Arthurian romances, which must have been recited by wandering storytellers before they were written down. In these romances—first written, as their name suggests, in a Romance language that had grown out of ancient Roman speech—the poets turned their backs upon the fiction of historical truth which the chroniclers had kept, and made Arthur and his retinue the centers of adventure and love stories suited to the taste of feudal courts. They described the manners and customs of a time when chivalry was flourishing and

The oldest known representation of Arthur. Detail of an early XII century carving on the cathedral of Modena. Inscribed: "Artus de Bretania"

when women held a high place in the life of court and castle, for the romancers set their stories in the background of their own day. The first certain representation of Arthur and his men in art dates from the twelfth century too. It is a crude carving over a doorway of the cathedral of Modena, in northern Italy, which represents some story of the abduction of Guenevere known there before the first romances were written—for the carving was probably done in the first half of the century. Only the names above the figures identify them. The king and his men wear long coats of mail and carry kite-shaped shields. Their attire is much more like that of William the Conqueror and his Normans than that probably worn by the half-Romanized warriors of Arthur's day.

Within a few years these romances had passed into all the languages of Europe, from Italy to Iceland. In the twelfth and early thirteenth centuries they were written in verse; those of later periods were chiefly in prose and were apt to be overloaded with complicated adventures. The most enduring of the romances were not merely tales of adventure, but were centered about themes akin to those which had inspired the tragedies of ancient Greece and were to dominate those of Shakespeare's day—in tragedies and romances alike, characters of high estate were doomed by their own actions to bring catastrophe.

The finest of all English romances of Arthur, Sir Thomas Malory's *Morte d'Arthur*, completed as late as 1469, was a compilation from several older sources. Al-

though the title, taken from a French romance, implies that the book deals only with Arthur's death, it begins before his birth and includes the adventures of his knights. In spite of the fact that it was drawn mainly from prose romances, which lacked much of the vivid simplicity of the earlier poems, and that its following of different sources often resulted in inconsistencies, Malory's book is a masterpiece of selective power, character portrayal, and prose style. Written in prison during the Wars of the Roses (1455-1485), which hastened English feudalism toward its end, this book was the outgrowth of one of those returns to an idealized heroic past which often occur in troubled times. In it Malory made a definite attempt to recall, through his description of heroic figures and noble deeds, the grandeur of the feudal England which was passing. He also suggested the conflicting loyalties which had led to the downfall of feudalism. William Caxton, who printed the *Morte d'Arthur* for the first time in 1485, pointed out both its dramatic qualities and its author's moral in his preface: "Herein may be seen noble chivalry, courtesy, humanity, friendliness, hardiness, love, friendship, cowardice, murder, hate, virtue, and sin. Do after the good and leave the evil, and it shall bring you to good fame and renown."

The year in which Malory's book was printed saw in England a new interest in Arthur, stimulated by the new king. Henry Tudor came to the throne as Henry VII in 1485 at the end of the Wars of the Roses. As part of his effort to conciliate all parties in England and also the Welsh, from whom he was descended on his father's side, he set about glorifying the ancient British hero. He claimed descent from Arthur and named his eldest son Arthur to suggest that king's return, declaring that Merlin's prophecy had now been fulfilled. The Round Table of heavy oak, eighteen feet in diameter, which hangs upon the wall of the great hall of Winchester Castle (illustrated opposite), was perhaps first decorated in its present style in honor of Prince Arthur's birth there in 1486, though the table itself is older. It was first mentioned about 1450 and may have been used in some forgotten tournament feast. Such festivals were sometimes called "Round Tables" after Arthur's famous board. The central rose of this table is the Tudor emblem, combining the white rose of York with the red of Lancaster. The radiating spokes are painted in the Tudor colors, green and white. A crudely painted figure of Arthur fills one compartment; in the others are the names of twenty-four knights, chiefly those found in Malory's book. Around the rose runs a circular band, inscribed: "Thys is the rownde table of Kyng Arthur w[ith] xxiiii of hys namyde knyghttes."

Mediaeval pictures of Arthur and his knights are found most frequently in illuminated manuscripts, but they also appear in wall paintings, sculpture, tapestries, carved ivory caskets and mirror cases, enameled vessels, and stained glass. Old inventories show that there were once many more of these, now lost. Comparatively few examples in painting and sculpture remain today and those that do are seldom the work of outstanding masters, for these usually devoted their time to religious subjects. During the Renaissance Arthurian romances went gradually out of fashion in both literature and art, though printed editions of the romances in the late fifteenth and sixteenth centuries introduced a new kind of picture—woodcut illustrations.

Long after the creative age of the romances was past, Arthurian stories remained well known in many forms both on the Continent and in England. In Italy they were blended with those of Charlemagne's paladins to form two of the outstanding poems of the Renaissance. Boiardo's *Orlando Innamorato*, composed soon after Malory's *Morte d'Arthur*, was on the border line between romance and epic. It told the adventures of the paladin Roland, or Orlando, changed into a knight-errant in an Arthurian setting. Ariosto's romantic epic, *Orlando Furioso*, printed in 1516, continued the story and gave Merlin an important part as a political prophet.

In England the stories of Arthur furnished subjects for pageants in Queen Elizabeth's time, both among the nobles whom she visited and among the citizens of London. The first Arthurian play in English, Thomas Hughes's *Misfortunes of Arthur*, was produced before the queen in 1588. Spenser used Arthur as one of the leading figures in his *Faerie Queene*; Ben Jonson's masque, *The Speeches at Prince Henry's Barriers*, was an Arthurian fantasy; and though none of Shakespeare's plays dealt with Arthurian personages, some of his English characters refer to them familiarly. But during the quarrel between the Stuart kings and Parliament in the seventeenth century Arthurian stories fell into disfavor, partly because they had been so closely connected with the kings and the royalist party. This was probably one reason why Milton did not write the epic he considered on "Arthur, who carried war into fairyland." The few Arthurian works of the second half of the seventeenth century reflect a less heroic period. Dryden had wished to write an epic on Arthur, but what he finally produced in 1691 was a political play, *King Arthur, the British Worthy*, with music by Purcell. The epic which he and Milton had each considered, was finally composed by Sir Richard Blackmore in his long and tedious *Prince Arthur*, published in 1695.

The stories of Arthur remained alive, however, in ballads and popular tales, even when they had ceased to be subjects of literary masterpieces. Arthur's court is the background of ballads such as that of *The Marriage of Sir Gawaine*, where

King Arthur lives in merry Carleile,
And semely is to see,
And there he hath with him Queene Genever,
That bride so bright of blee.

And there he hath with him Queene Genever,
That bride so bright in bower.
And all his barons about him stoode,
That were both stiff and stowre.

The king's court, too, was the background for popular stories like Tom Thumb and Jack the Giant Killer, which were widely read as chapbooks and retold as nursery fairy tales.

The early eighteenth century was generally scornful of such stories as those of Arthur and his knights, feeling that the world had reached an age of reason and common sense in which heroic legends had no place. The only Arthurian work by a well-known writer of this time was Fielding's play *The Life and Death of Tom Thumb the Great*, taken from a chapbook which had its setting in Arthur's court. As might be expected, this was a burlesque of the fashionable, ranting tragedies of the period. But before the century was over there was a reawakened interest in the mediaeval past. One of the most important expressions of this interest was the publication in 1765 of a collection of poems and ballads, Percy's *Reliques of Ancient English Poetry*. This book, which included *The Marriage of Sir Gawaine* and five other Arthurian pieces, made many readers familiar with the old, half-forgotten stories.

By the 1830's interest in the Middle Ages had become widespread in England, the country which had led the world in industrial development, but where social discontent was leading toward a new valuation of the past. For this discontent there were many reasons. The invention of the steam engine and other promising scientific discoveries of the late eighteenth century had brought disappointments. Larger production had not made the world happier. The inclosure of common lands to encourage farming on a large scale had almost destroyed the independent small farmers of England and had reduced many to the state of day laborers at a starvation wage. The general shift from farming to industry had wiped out the old relationships between men, and new ones had not risen to take their place. Power machines had made some men slaves, leaving others without work, and had widened and made more noticeable the gulf between rich and poor. Under these circumstances the minds of many Englishmen turned toward the Middle Ages, which seemed to show the stability their own time lacked. There was some basis of fact for this idealized picture of English history, but distance veiled many less pleasing things.

Some religious leaders looked back with regret to the universal Church of the Middle Ages, in which all men

The great hall of Winchester Castle. The Round Table on the wall may have been first decorated in its present style in 1486. The Table also appears on the cover

were brothers in a single faith that had not been shaken by scientific theories. This feeling gave rise to the Oxford movement for church reform, which took its name from the university to which many of its leaders belonged. Besides working for reform within the Church of England, this movement revived much of the beautiful mediaeval liturgy, the church furnishings which went with it, and the Gothic style in church buildings.

Political leaders, too, looked to the past for inspiration. Some Conservatives, led by Disraeli, and known as the "Young England" group, favored a strong monarchy and something like the social relationships of feudalism in industry. Others of a more radical turn, among them William Cobbett, drew unfavorable comparisons between farm workers in the nineteenth century and in the Middle Ages. The weakness of the trade unions in the early nineteenth century, when assemblies of laborers to discuss working conditions were illegal, could also be compared unfavorably with the power of the mediaeval industrial guilds.

7

Sir Galahad. Pen drawing by Edward Burne-Jones, 1858-1859. Fogg Museum of Art, Harvard University

In English literature this interest in the Middle Ages led to a revival of mediaeval subjects in general and to the first wide use of Arthurian stories in three centuries. Tennyson began to experiment with these legends in his *Lady of Shalott*, published in 1832. In 1842 appeared his short poems *Sir Launcelot and Queen Guinevere* and *Sir Galahad* and his longer *Morte d'Arthur*. Ten years later Matthew Arnold published his *Tristram and Iseult*. Among the short poems of William Morris, printed in 1858, were several on Arthurian themes, including *The Defence of Guenevere, King Arthur's Tomb*, and *Sir Galahad, a Christmas Mystery*. Tennyson's *Idylls of the King*, the most widely known of all nineteenth-century Arthurian poems, were issued between 1859 and 1885. Swinburne's *Tristram of Lyonesse* was published in 1882. Arthurian subjects have been carried on in twentieth-century English poetry by Hardy's *Tragedy of the Queen of Cornwall* and by Masefield's *Tristan and Isolt* and the short Arthurian poems of his *Midsummer Night*.

Malory's *Morte d'Arthur* was the chief source of inspiration for Arthurian poetry and art in nineteenth-century England. Poets and artists found in it a masterpiece of English prose, which they ranked with the King James translation of the Bible. They also recognized in Malory's interpretation of the old romances something akin to their own yearning toward a heroic past. His stories appealed both to the nationalistic spirit, which was strong in England after the Napoleonic wars, and to the hunger for a personal hero and a common bond of fellowship. These men interpreted the old legends in the light of their own times, using them as mirrors to reflect contemporary ideas and standards and altering details to accomplish this purpose.

The Gothic revival in architecture was the first evidence in art of the new interest in the Middle Ages, but the other arts followed before long. In the late 1840's a group of young English painters rebelled against studying art by copying antique sculpture and the works of Raphael. Their leaders were Dante Gabriel Rossetti, John Everett Millais, and Holman Hunt; their ranks were soon joined by others, among the most notable of whom were Edward Burne-Jones and William Morris, the latter better known as a poet, craftsman, and socialist than as a painter. Because of their admiration for mediaeval and early Renaissance work these artists were commonly called "Pre-Raphaelites," although they did not intend to copy the painters before Raphael's day any more than they wished to copy the master himself. They were also attracted by themes from mediaeval literature and history because they found among them many of the "great and ennobling subjects" which they felt it was an artist's duty to portray. Some of their mannerisms of drawing and composition did indeed suggest the art of the Middle Ages. They did not, for instance, make much use of deep perspective; most of them had a passion for detail; and they sometimes produced an effect of naïve awkwardness not unlike that of mediaeval painting by their insistence upon fidelity to nature rather than formal planning of composition. In their own right, however, the Pre-Raphaelites made a distinctive contribution both to art and to the interpretation of the Arthurian legends. The charm of their work is neither mediaeval nor modern, but belongs to a dream world, beyond space and time.

Rossetti and Burne-Jones, who were among the more poetic members of the group, were especially drawn toward the Arthurian romances which were inspiring the poets of their time. Burne-Jones's drawing of Sir Galahad shows not only the Pre-Raphaelite characteristics of flatness and elaborate detail, but also the close relationship between literature and art typical of this school. It bears the stamp of the two outstanding nineteenth-century painters of the Arthurian legends, for the figures of the lovers in the background closely resemble those by the artist's friend and teacher, Rossetti, and Galahad himself shows the wistful, idealized features and delicate modeling which mark Burne-Jones's later work. Tennyson's *Sir Galahad*, which suggests the contrast between earthly love at Arthur's court and the Grail knight's own austere life, has been called the inspiration of the drawing. But this idea had been developed much more fully and emphatically by the artist's close friend, Morris, in his *Sir Galahad*, published in 1858, about the time the drawing was done. Tennyson had been inspired by Malory; Morris and Burne-Jones were influenced by Malory, Tennyson, and each other. All three expressed a strong, popular interest in subjects from romance, such as had not existed since the Middle Ages, so that whether the picture or the poems came first makes little difference.

In Germany as in England discontent with existing circumstances led poets and artists to seek inspiration in their own national mediaeval literature. Arthurian romance found there a new artistic expression in Wagner's operas. Wagner took from the old German romances of Tristan and Parzival the themes for his *Tristan and Isolde* and *Parsifal*, in which the music of orchestra and voice shaped fresh beauty about the old stories.

Although social conditions in the United States were very different from those in Europe, the interest in Arthurian stories was shared by Americans, who looked to the Old World for intellectual and artistic leadership. Malory's romance and the body of fairy tales and ballads were the common literary heritage of England and America, and American critics, poets, and teachers were friends and admirers of contemporary British poets. These old and new sources of Arthurian stories were pointed out in the note which James Russell Lowell published with his *Vision of Sir Launfal* in 1848. After outlining briefly the story of the Grail, he wrote: "Sir Galahad was at last successful in finding it, as may be read in the seventeenth book of the Romance of King Arthur [Malory's *Morte d'Arthur*]. Tennyson has made Sir Galahad the subject of one of the most exquisite of his poems." Lowell's poem, in spite of its inspiration and theme, was not strictly Arthurian; for Launfal was a creation of the poet's fancy, with a name from French romance, and there is no mention of Arthur or any of his knights of the Round Table.

Tennyson's popularity in America increased rapidly after the publication of the volume of 1842 containing the *Sir Galahad* to which Lowell referred. *The Idylls of the King* reached an immense public, and at least as early as the 1890's some of them were being taught in the public schools—a practice which soon became general. Probably no other single means ever built up so large a group of people familiar with Arthur and the Round Table as this use in schools, over a long period of time, of the *Idylls* and other forms of Arthurian stories.

The humorous treatment of these stories in Mark Twain's *Connecticut Yankee in King Arthur's Court*, published in 1889, was characteristic of nineteenth-century America. Late in the century Richard Hovey wrote several serious Arthurian plays and masques in verse, but no poetry on these themes comparable to English works appeared in this country until 1917. In this year Edwin Arlington Robinson published his *Merlin*; in 1920 there followed his *Lancelot*, and in 1927 his *Tristram*. Robinson's poems take for granted a knowledge of the stories and make no attempt to recreate a mediaeval world. They plunge at once into analysis of character and events treated as timeless and enduring themes. Writing near the end of the first World War and in the shadow of the second, Robinson's interpretation was that of a man profoundly moved by the disillusionments and uncertainties of the period, and he used the fate of Arthur and his Round Table as

a mirror wherein men
May see themselves, and pause. . . .

BELOW: *The heraldic arms of Sir Tristan, from The Names, Arms, and Blazons of the Knights of the Round Table. French manuscript, about 1500. In the Pierpont Morgan Library, New York, M16, fol. 29*

Scenes from the story of Lancelot painted on castle walls. Manuscript illumination, about 1470, from a French prose romance of Lancelot. In the Bibliothèque Nationale, Paris, Fr. 112, vol. III, fol. 193

CASTLES PAINTED WITH ARTHURIAN SCENES

Mediaeval literature contains many descriptions of castle walls painted with scenes from romances. The prose romance of Lancelot, for instance, tells that the hero, imprisoned by Morgan le Fay because he had refused her love, passed his time in painting upon the walls of his room scenes showing how he "was abashed at the great beauty of his lady when that he first saw her" and the happenings at "the tourney when he wore the red armour, the day when the King of the Hundred Knights wounded him." In the manuscript illumination above Arthur is studying these frescoes, which the jealous Morgan showed him. Not content with painting the scenes, Lancelot had also added inscriptions identifying them and making unmistakably clear his love for Arthur's queen. Such inscriptions still accompany some of the actual wall paintings which exist today—in the castle of Saint-Floret, for instance, or at La Manta or Castle Runkelstein.

Boccaccio's *Amorosa Visione*, written about 1342, has a famous description of imaginary Arthurian paintings on the walls of the allegorical castle of Mundane Life: "King Arthur was among the first there, riding in front upon a great destrier, armed at all points, fierce and proud. Bors followed spurring close after him, and with him Perceval and Galahad at a slow pace, talking together. Behind them came Lancelot armed and gracious of carriage, a lance in his hand, uttering no word, often striking his powerful horse in order to be near the

sweet lady whom to touch seemed to him the end of desire. How beautiful and how excellent was she! At his side came Guinevere upon a palfrey, smiling in manner, full of grace, holding sweet converse with him in silent, sober words. She was with him for whose sake she had lived in joy, loving him long and without measure, even though afterward she wept therefor. . . . Close behind came good Tristram upon a mighty and swift horse; Ysolt the Blonde came beside him, his hand clasped in hers, often looking into his face. How anguished was her visage by the power of love, with which all the soul within her seemed to burn, so that it shed light through all her outward acts."

The paintings of Arthurian stories which still remain on a few castle walls show no such sympathetic treatment or suggestion of emotion as Boccaccio's description. Even the greatest painters of the time—Giotto, Simone Martini, and Pietro and Ambrogio Lorenzetti—could scarcely have conveyed the passion which the poet could express in words. But neither then nor in the fifteenth century were the greatest painters likely to be employed upon the castles whose walls still show paintings of Arthur and his knights. The castles which have kept their mediaeval decorations most unspoiled are those of the lesser nobles or wealthy citizens, situated in remote, quiet places—castles whose owners could not command the services of master painters from the great cities. The châteaux and town dwellings of kings and powerful nobles, who might have employed such artists to paint their palace walls, have been redecorated and changed to follow the fashions of the times, and if any Arthurian paintings ever existed in them they were destroyed or hidden long ago.

The most complete remaining example of a mediaeval castle with wall paintings from Arthurian romance is Castle Runkelstein, or Roncolo, as it is called by Italians, shown opposite. It stands on a steep porphyry crag overlooking the swiftly flowing Talfer, near Bolzano, in southern Tyrol, where the foothills of the Alps begin to rise toward the Brenner Pass. This castle, founded in 1237, was bought in 1385 by Niklas Vintner, a Tyrolese banker, and his brother Franz. Niklas probably finished his building and redecorating by 1400. His interest in Arthurian stories must have been great, for he decorated his new wing, the Summer House on the north side of the open courtyard, chiefly with scenes from German versions of these romances.

The view of Runkelstein opposite shows the cliff and terraced vineyards rising above the Talfer, with the steep, narrow path which is its only approach wind-

*Castle Runkelstein near Bolzano in Tyrol. The Summer
House, painted with Arthurian stories, is at the left.
Some of the paintings are shown on pages 13, 21, 40, 41*

The courtyard of Castle Runkelstein, looking toward the Summer House. The open loggia, balcony, and upper rooms were painted about 1400

ing at the right. The dark, oblong window below the crenelated battlements looks out from the courtyard across the vineyards. To the left of the window is the red-tiled roof of Niklas Vintner's Summer House, with a chimney rising from the room in which is painted the story of Garel. The outer wall of the courtyard and the tall building at its right belong to the thirteenth-century castle. Within this old building, known as the West Palace, are other wall paintings made for Niklas Vintner —tournaments and rows of slender lords and ladies dancing the carol—but these have no connection with Arthur. After the death of Niklas in 1413 the castle passed to his brother Franz and then from one owner to another until it came into the possession of the Emperor Maximilian about 1500. With his passion for romance and knightly adventures he was naturally much interested in the paintings, and between 1503 and 1511 he sent three court painters to restore them. The results were unfortunate, for the sixteenth-century work does not harmonize with the earlier compositions which it covers. The greatest changes were made in the Summer House rooms painted with the stories of Garel and Tristan; the fres-

coes which did not have romance subjects have been less repainted, and look much as their late fourteenth-century painters left them—filled with slender, courtly figures of great elegance and grace, though damaged by time and long neglect. About the middle of the nineteenth century the castle was presented to the Austrian emperor Franz Josef, who restored it and in 1893 gave it to the town of Bolzano.

The picture above shows the courtyard of the castle and the Summer House. In the courtyard the citizens of Bolzano, not so long ago, held concerts and ate and drank. The walls and piers of the loggia opening off the court were painted in grayish green monochrome with scenes from the story of Wigalois, or Guiglain, the son of Gawain, as told by an Austrian poet. They have been so badly damaged by weather that little now remains. The paintings on the covered balcony above are in better condition, but they also are much scratched and worn. On this balcony the mediaeval taste for classified groups ran riot. On the outer wall, under the protecting roof, are groups of characters from legend and romance, arranged in threes. From left to right these are: the Nine Worthies, who will be met again (pages 28-30); three Knights of the Round Table—Perceval, Gawain, and Ywain; three pairs of famous lovers—William of Austria and Aglei, Tristan and Iseult, and William of Orleans

A room in the Summer House at Runkelstein painted with the story of Garel. Beside the chimney at the left is the Round Table fresco shown on page 21

and Amaley; three heroes of German epic and folk tale—Dietrich of Bern, Siegfried, and Dietlieb of Styria; the three strongest giants; and the three wildest giantesses. Arthur's figure is worn and blurred as he sits among the Worthies, carrying a scepter in his hand. Perceval bears upon his shield a silver anchor on a red ground, Gawain a white hart, and Ywain a spread eagle. Tristan, in a light red robe, clasps the hand of Iseult, who is dressed in a trailing gown of blue. Above him is his shield, bearing the image of a boar—the arms described by Gottfried von Strassburg, which recall his fame as a hunter. A more usual device was a lion rampant, suggesting the name of his land of Lyonesse.

The story painted on the walls of the Garel room, shown above, on the second floor of the Summer House, is only loosely connected with Arthur. Garel is a prince of Styria, or Steiermark, in the thirteenth-century Austrian romance of *Garel of the Blossoming Vale*, which furnished the subject for the painter. He is a nephew of Arthur in this story, as Gareth is in the French and English romances, but that, and the fact that he brings the kings whom he captures to Arthur's court, are the only connections this romance has with the British king.

The scenes in this room have a special interest because they include the oldest surviving wall painting of the Round Table (illustrated on page 21). In the view above

this appears in the corner next the chimney. All the scenes are shown against a background of warm red and glow with somber richness in the dimly lighted room, even after the ravages of repainting and more than five centuries of wear. Some of the paintings on the north wall and some from the Tristan room next door were destroyed when a part of the wall fell in 1868. A row of biblical portraits framed by painted arches runs beneath the Garel scenes, and below these is a painted decoration imitating figured cloth—a very common way of decorating the lower parts of walls, exposed to the hardest wear.

On a hill near the town of Saluzzo, in the Piedmont section of northern Italy, rises the castle of La Manta. In its great hall, decorated for Valerano and Clemensia Provana about 1430, Arthur appears with the popular mediaeval group of the Nine Worthies. The interior of this hall is illustrated on page 15. Two of the Worthies, Hector of Troy and Alexander the Great, are shown beside the chimney, at the right, in this view. Arthur's figure is the fifth from the right on the side wall. The immediate source of these paintings was a French poem, *Le*

The castle of La Manta near Saluzzo in northern Italy.
Arthur is shown among the Nine Worthies in one of its
rooms, decorated about 1430

Chevalier errant, written early in the fifteenth century
by Valerano Provana's father, the Duke of Saluzzo, who
had lived in France and was steeped in French culture.
In the poem the hero comes to the Palace of Fortune and
sees there the thrones of the Nine Worthies and the Nine
Worthy Ladies.

The last two figures on the right wall belong to the
group of Nine Worthy Ladies. The nine women were
not so invariable a group as the nine men, but those
chosen by the Duke of Saluzzo and painted on the wall
at La Manta were generally popular and were often represented in tapestries. They were not ladies of romance
but Amazons or warrior queens. Some were well known
in classical writings, others were drawn from the later
Latin histories which were favorites in the Middle Ages.
Deipylé, or Delfilé, and Sinope are the two shown above.
The others were Lampeto, Semiramis, Tomyris, Teuca,

Penthesilea, Hippolyta, and Melanippe—all women of
the ancient, pagan world. Later, Joan of Arc was sometimes added to their number. The names and deeds of
the Nine Ladies are inscribed in French verses below
them, to match the Nine Worthies, and they also have
shields bearing appropriate arms. The Ladies' garments
are even more extravagantly fantastic than those of the
Worthies. Their trailing sleeves, often with deep points
or scallops, and their elaborate headdresses resemble
those of costumes in French and Flemish miniatures of
the time.

On the left-hand wall are continuous scenes present-
ing a fancy dear to many ages—the Fountain of Youth.
All classes and conditions of men and women ride or
limp toward the fountain, an elaborate Gothic structure
just visible at the left. Upon reaching it, they plunge
into its waters and emerge with renewed youth. The
scene on the end wall, next to the chimney, shows the
last of the rejuvenated persons riding gaily away. The
lower part of the wall is painted to resemble figured
cloth.

The castle of Saint-Floret, near Issoire in Auvergne,

A room in the castle of La Manta painted with the Nine Worthies, the Nine Worthy Ladies, and the Fountain of Youth. Arthur is the fifth figure from the right

illustrated on page 16, also has paintings from romance. The great hall in the square tower of this French castle is decorated with damaged but lovely frescoes of the story of Tristan and Iseult, painted about 1350. The scene of Tristan and Iseult at the fountain is shown on pages 44 and 45. Galahad is painted here, too, with his red-cross shield, and other knights whose adventures are told in the prose romances of Tristan. There is also a queen, with attendant ladies, who is probably Guenevere. The fact that this hall was used for years as a barn and threshing floor saved it from the redecoration given to castles which were continuously lived in and kept in repair; it also accounts for much weathering and many scratches. The paintings were discovered soon after 1860, and in 1930 the castle was bought by the State to insure the safety of the remaining frescoes.

Castle Rhäzüns, near Chur in the Swiss canton of Graubünden, has a room painted with the most popular of mediaeval romance scenes—the meeting of Tristan and Iseult at the fountain. This painting is illustrated on page 43. The castle itself, shown on page 17, stands upon a steep, wooded rock near a branch of the Rhine.

A few Arthurian paintings remain in other castles. Arthur appears among the Nine Worthies in late fifteenth-century frescoes at the castle of Valeria at Sion, Switzerland, and remnants of thirteenth-century paintings of the story of Ywain, Knight of the Lion, as told by Chrétien de Troyes, are still in a ground-floor room of a house in the town of Schmalkalden in Thuringia. Scenes from the romance of Tristan and Iseult, among other subjects from romance and fantasy, are shown in the fourteenth-century wooden ceiling in the Chiaramonte Palace in Palermo. The lovers in the Forest of Morrois, from this ceiling, are shown on page 46. Considering the many descriptions of such paintings in mediaeval literature, those mentioned seem only a small group; but more pictures of Arthur and his knights may still be hidden beneath whitewash or paint, waiting to be discovered.

*The castle of Saint-Floret near Issoire in Auvergne. Wall
paintings of Tristan and Iseult painted here about 1350
are shown on pages 44 and 45*

Castle Rhäzüns near Chur in the Swiss canton of Grau-
bünden or Grisons. A wall painting of Tristan and
Iseult in this castle is shown on page 43

KING ARTHUR AND HIS COURT

Although King Arthur's adventures were often overshadowed by those of his knights, a few scenes from his life were repeated over and over in both literature and art for centuries. Such a story is that of Arthur's youth and coming to the throne. When Arthur was born, King Uther, his father, gave him into the hands of the enchanter Merlin, who had him brought up ignorant of his true identity by the noble knight Sir Ector de Maris. After Uther's death there was great strife in England—the land of Logres, as the romances called it. Finally, says Malory, there appeared in the churchyard of "the greatest church of London, whether it were Paul's or not the French book maketh no mention, . . . a great stone four square, like unto a marble stone, and in the midst thereof was like an anvil of steel a foot on high, and therein stuck a fair sword naked by the point, and letters there were written in gold about the sword that said thus:—Whoso pulleth out this sword of this stone and anvil, is rightwise king born of all England." Many a noble tried his hand, but none could move it. This sword was not Excalibur, which Arthur found later.

On New Year's Day a great joust was held in London, in which Arthur's foster brother, Sir Kay, found himself unable to take part, as he had wished to do, because he had left his sword behind. Blunders of this sort and a complete lack of any sense of humor later made Kay the comic figure among the knights, perpetually getting into trouble. Young Arthur rode back to bring the sword, but found that everyone had gone out to see the

jousting. Remembering the sword in the stone, he set out to get it, saying, "My brother Sir Kay shall not be without a sword this day." He pulled it out easily and bore it to Kay, who recognized it and took it to his father, declaring, "Sir, lo here is the sword of the stone, wherefore I must be king of this land." Sir Ector, who knew his son, took both youths to the churchyard; there Arthur put the sword back into the stone and pulled it out easily, but Kay could not move it. "Therewithal they went unto the Archbishop, and told him how the sword was achieved, and by whom; and on Twelfth-day all the barons came thither" to try the sword again. Still none could move it, and they assembled at Candlemas and the Feast of Pentecost with the same result, though each time Arthur drew the sword easily. Finally, "all the commons cried at once, We will have Arthur unto our king, we will put him no more in delay, for we all see that it is God's will that he shall be our king, and who that holdeth against it, we will slay him." So Arthur "took the sword between both his hands, and offered it upon the altar where the Archbishop was, and so was he made knight of the best man that was there. And so anon was the coronation made. And there was he sworn unto his lords and the commons for to be a true king, to stand with true justice from thenceforth the days of this life." The emphasis upon the "lords and the commons" is distinctly English, re-

flecting the slow growth of parliamentary power in England through more than two centuries. The Wars of the Roses, in which Malory took part, not only hastened the decline of mediaeval chivalry but also checked the growth of Parliament. In the upper band of the illumination at the left on the opposite page, Arthur is drawing the sword; in the lower band, he is laying it upon the altar while the archbishop places a crown upon his head. The backgrounds are bright gold, and the gay-robed knights and clergy seem as boyish as Arthur himself.

Stories of Arthur's prowess in battle were also common, though the king became more and more the central, administrative figure rather than the hero, and many of his own knights could outfight him. The battle scene on the opposite page shows Arthur, early in his reign, fighting a group of rebellious kings who refused to recognize "a beardless boy" as their overlord. All the warriors are clad in mail with flowing surcoats and Arthur wears a crown over his closed helmet. A knight beside him carries a winged scarlet dragon, the battle standard of King Uther. Geoffrey of Monmouth says that Uther had this made because of a vision of a dragon which Merlin interpreted favorably. He kept it, says Geoffrey, "to carry about with him in the wars. From that day forth was he called Uther Pendragon, for thus do we call a dragon's head in the British tongue."

Geoffrey's story of Arthur and the Giant of Mont-St.-Michel was also repeated in the romances. The miniature of Arthur and the giant, however, is from an abridged version of Wace's chronicle. The king had come to the rocky island off the coast of Normandy, where now the great abbey stands, to avenge the daughter of his ally, the king of Brittany, for the giant had carried the maiden away and killed her. Wace says: "Now when Arthur drew near to the summit of the mount, he beheld the giant crouched above his fire. He broiled a hog within the flame upon a spit. Part of the flesh he had eaten already, and part of the meat was charred and burning in the fire. He was the more hideous to see because his beard and hair were foul with blood and coal." The giant fought savagely, but finally "the king smote him so fiercely with Excalibur that the blade clove to his brain and he fell." The picture has much of the rough realism of the story but is lightened by the presence of the rabbits darting in and out of their burrows, undisturbed by the giant. Arthur's features are very like those of the sturdy yeomen in English paintings of the time, and the picture as a whole is more like an illustration of the fairy tale of Jack the Giant Killer than a scene from a courtly chronicle.

Merlin the enchanter was one of the most important figures of Arthur's court. Half human and half demon, Merlin knew past and future and the magic spells of every land and time. Men said that he had brought the mighty rocks of Stonehenge from Ireland to England. The miniature of the moving of Stonehenge is perhaps the earliest picture of this ancient monument. According to Wace, Aurelius, Uther's brother, wished to erect a worthy monument to his men who had been killed in battle, and Merlin suggested this "mighty circle of

stones," brought from Africa by a giant. Uther's men were sent to fetch it, but they found that, though they heaved and tugged, the stones "would not budge one single inch." Then Merlin "entered within the carol. He walked warily around the stones. His lips moved without stay, as those of a man about his orisons, though I cannot tell whether or no he prayed." After this incantation the men lifted the stones like pebbles and bore them to England, where Merlin ranged them "in due order, building them side by side. This circle of stones was called by the Britons in their own tongue, The Giant's Carol, but in English it bears the name of Stonehenge." And there both Aurelius and Uther Pendragon were buried. Geoffrey of Monmouth and Layamon tell practically the same story.

The woodcut from the first illustrated edition of Malory's *Morte d'Arthur* shows Merlin's doom as the English romancer related it. The aged enchanter had become so enamored of Nimue, one of the damsels of the Lake, that he could not bear her out of his sight. He knew that this passion would bring him to his end, but he was powerless to avert his own fate. The damsel finally grew tired of him—and afraid. She besought him to teach her his magic spells, and he could not deny her. Then, as Malory tells the story, "On a time it happened that Merlin showed to her in a rock whereas was a great wonder, and wrought by enchantment, that went under a great stone. So by her subtle working she made Merlin to go under that stone to let her wit of the marvels there, but she wrought so there for him that he came never out for all the craft he could do. And so she departed and left Merlin."

Other stories of Merlin's end are different. A thirteenth-century French romance, which was translated into English about 1450 to 1460, says that Nimue loved Merlin deeply and was afraid that she might lose him. So she begged him to teach her how to build a magic tower of air. One day the two went hand in hand through the Forest of Broceliande and sat down to rest by a fair hawthorn bush full of sweet white flowers. There Merlin fell asleep with his head in Nimue's lap, and while he slept she softly made a circle with her wimple about the bush. When Merlin woke, "him seemed that he was in the fairest tower of the world and the most strong;—and he said to the damsel: Lady ye have me deceived, but if ye will abide with me, for none but ye may undo this enchantment." And because the damsel loved him she spent most of her time in the magic tower.

Merlin's name was naturally linked with Arthur's Round Table, which was famous throughout Europe. Wace, who was the first to mention it, says that the king founded the Round Table so "that when his fair fellowship sat to meat their chairs should be high alike, their service equal, and none before or after his comrade." An early Merlin romance says that the table was made for Uther Pendragon by Merlin's advice, to commemorate the Table of the Last Supper. According to Malory, "Merlin made the Round Table in tokening of the roundness of the world." Later it came into the possession of Guenevere's father, who sent it to Arthur as a wedding gift, and Merlin helped the king to find knights to fill it. At this table the knights' names were written in letters of gold, but one seat, the Siege Perilous, remained vacant for the Good Knight who was to come. As Merlin foretold, disaster overtook anyone else who sat in it.

The Round Table fresco on the opposite page, painted at Castle Runkelstein about 1400, is the oldest large painting of this subject which remains. The table is set in a meadow under a spreading tree. Arthur sits in front of its trunk with his nephew Garel at his right. The king's device, the three crowns of England, Scotland, and Brittany, show faintly on the pennant floating from the trumpet near his head. The background of the painting is a warm red.

Some of the outstanding figures of Arthur's court had their own cycles of romance, more or less closely connected with the great king. The story of Lancelot and Guenevere, though it formed an inseparable part of the history of Arthur, was developed in the cycle of Lancelot romances. Tristan and Galahad, too, had their

Arthur's Round Table. Wall painting, about 1400. In the Summer House at Castle Runkelstein, near Bolzano

The return of Excalibur. Manuscript illumination, about 1316, from a French prose romance. In the British Museum, Add. MS 10294, fol. 94

own romances, sometimes connected very loosely with those of Arthur. But all the cycles were united by the fact that their heroes finally became knights of the Round Table.

While the adventures of these heroes fill the stage, Arthur plays a small and sometimes unattractive part. But at the end of his life, as at its beginning, the great king is the hero of the story. Merlin was gone; Galahad had achieved the Grail and died; Gawain was dead; Lancelot was in exile because of Guenevere; and the treacherous Mordred, Arthur's illegitimate son, had rebelled while Arthur was in France fighting with Lancelot. Malory makes it clear that this conflict with Mordred was the outcome of the king's past error. Nevertheless he comments sadly upon the fickleness of Arthur's subjects in siding with Mordred as a parallel to the swift changing of sides in his own England during the Wars of the Roses: "Lo ye all Englishmen, see ye not what mischief here was! for he that was the most king and knight of the world, and most loved the fellowship of noble knights, and by him they were all upholden, now might not these Englishmen hold them content with him. Lo thus was the old custom and usage of this land; and also men say that we of this land have not yet lost nor forgotten that custom and usage. Alas, this is a great default of us Englishmen, for there may no thing please us no term. And so fared the people at that time, they were better pleased with Sir Mordred than they were with King Arthur."

When the last battle by the sea was over, Mordred and all his men lay dead, and Arthur, sorely wounded, was left alone with Sir Bedivere. Then said the king:

"Take thou Excalibur, my good sword, and go with it to yonder water side, and when thou comest there I charge thee throw my sword into that water, and come again and tell me what thou there seest." Bedivere took the sword, but he could not bring himself to cast away so goodly a blade. So he hid it and told Arthur that he had done his command. But when he was questioned as to what he had seen and he replied, "I saw nothing but waves and winds," Arthur knew that this was not the truth. Again the king sent Bedivere to the waterside, and again Bedivere reported that he had cast away the sword but had seen "nothing but the waters wappe and the waves wanne." Once more the king reproached him and told him that this delay might be fatal, and at last Bedivere did as he had been commanded. "He bound the girdle about the hilts, and then he threw the sword as far into the water, as he might; and there came an arm and an hand above the water and met it, and caught it, and so shook it thrice and brandished, and then vanished away the hand with the sword in the water. So Sir Bedivere came again to the king, and told him what he saw. Alas, said the king, help me hence, for I dread me I have tarried over long. Then Sir Bedivere took the king upon his back, and so went with him to that water side. And when they were at the water side, even fast by the bank hoved a little barge with many fair ladies in it, and among them all was a queen, and all they had black hoods, and all they wept and shrieked when they saw King Arthur. Now put me into the barge, said the king. And so he did softly; and there received him three queens with great mourning; and so they set them down, and in one of their laps King Arthur laid his head. And then that queen said: Ah, dear brother, why have ye tarried so long from me? Alas, this wound on your head hath caught over-much cold. And so then they rowed from the land, and Sir Bedivere beheld all those ladies go from him. Then Sir Bedivere cried: Ah, my lord Arthur what shall become of me, now ye go from me and leave me here alone among mine enemies? Comfort thyself, said the king, and do as well as thou mayest, for in me is no trust for to trust in; for I will into the vale of Avilion to heal me of my grievous wound: and if thou hear never more of me, pray for my soul."

In the morning Bedivere came upon a fresh-made grave in a little chapel, and a hermit told him that there lay a body brought at midnight by women. "Alas, said Sir Bedivere, that was my lord King Arthur, that here lieth buried in this chapel." "More of the very certainty of his death heard I never read," says Malory, "but thus was he led away in a ship wherein were three queens; that one was King Arthur's sister, Queen Morgan le Fay; the other was the Queen of Northgalis; the third was the Queen of the Waste Lands. Also there was Nimue, the chief lady of the lake. . . . More of the death of King Arthur could I never find, but that ladies

per lo mare vna nauicella sepresse loro Artuso, vesibelmente eportollo via p lomare

elo sacerro como grande piquera tanto lo miro quanto ello pote e poi se diparti e andossene asia via dicendo la maluasia nonella laqnale era mtramennita allo re Artueo sno sieque

brought him to his burials. . . . Yet some men say in many parts of England that King Arthur is not dead, but had by the will of our Lord Jesu into another place; and men say that he shall come again, and he shall win the holy cross. I will not say it shall be so, but rather I will say, here in this world he changed his life. But many men say that there is written upon his tomb this verse: HIC JACET ARTHURUS REX, QUONDAM REX QUE FUTURUS [Here lieth Arthur, king that was and king that shall be]."

The little miniature opposite does less than justice to the majestic close of the story. Yet it suggests the loneliness of the marshy shore where Arthur waits disconsolate for the coming of the barge summoned by the casting away of Excalibur, while the great arm brandishes the sword thrown into the lake.

The pen drawing above, from an Italian romance of the Round Table, has more of the delicate charm of fairy tale. Arthur and his last knight seem like grave and lovely children playing some mysterious game. After the fashion of mediaeval narrative art, the unearthly arm brandishing Excalibur is shown in the same scene as Arthur's passing. While delightful waterfowl play along the shore the barge leaps on its way across the

The passing of Arthur to Avalon. Pen drawing, North Italian, 1446, from an Italian prose romance of the Round Table. Biblioteca Nazionale, Florence, Cod. Pal. 556

curly waves, guided by no mortal hand. In this Italian romance Arthur was not accompanied by weeping queens on his voyage to Avalon: after the arm had taken Excalibur beneath the water "there came over the sea a small boat, all covered with white, and, when King Arthur saw it, he said to the squire: Now has come mine end. And the ship drew near the king, and from the ship came forth some arms that took King Arthur and visibly set him in the ship, and bore him away over the sea. And the squire, greatly terrified, stayed there as long as he could see the ship; then he departed, and related the marvel. And it is believed that Morgan le Fay came by art in that little ship, and bore him away to an island of the sea, and there he died of his wounds, and the Fay buried him in that island." The island is not named in this romance. But Malory said that the chapel to which the women brought a body at midnight was near Glastonbury, where the tombs of Arthur and Guenevere were shown. And legend identified Glastonbury, ringed by watery fens, as the fairy isle of Avalon itself.

A tournament before Arthur outside Camelot. Detail of a manuscript illumination, 1463, from a French prose romance of Tristan. In the Bibliothèque Nationale, Paris, Fr. 99, fol. 561

Tournaments and jousts, filled with the clash of arms and gorgeous trappings, formed the background of life at Arthur's court. The miniature above shows the tournament held after Galahad's first appearance at court, when Arthur summoned all his knights "together in the meadow of Camelot to joust and to tourney" and to see Galahad prove his skill. Galahad is the central figure, bearing no shield or heraldic device, for he had not yet found the white shield blazoned with a red cross which had been awaiting him for centuries, and he refused to bear another. The other knights are gay with armorial devices, and Arthur's golden crowns are embroidered on the blue hanging which drapes the stand where he and the ladies of the court sit to watch the contest.

Tournaments actually began much later than the historic Arthur's day—perhaps in the eleventh century. They were very popular in the second half of the twelfth century, when the first romances were written, and since the romancers portrayed Arthur's followers as knights of their own time, tournaments were given a large place in their accounts of the activities of the Round Table.

Women played an important part in these trials of masculine strength and skill. They not only watched with admiring interest, but presented the prizes and sometimes acted as judges, for a knowledge of the fine points of tourney and joust was part of an accomplished lady's education. Often a knight wore his lady's favor, such as a sleeve, glove, kerchief, or veil, upon his arm or crest and declared that he sought glory for her sake alone.

The purpose of tournaments and jousts was to keep knights in training for the warfare which was their serious business in life, and to give them an opportunity to win glory and renown in peace. A tournament was a mock battle between two troops of knights. A joust was a contest between individuals, in which each tried to splinter the greatest number of lances in the most correct fashion or, if possible, to unhorse his opponent. The word tournament, however, was often used to include both. Lances were the most common weapons, especially in jousts, but swords and axes were also used.

These sports involved considerable danger, and as time went on the tilt, or barrier, was invented as a safety measure. This was originally a cloth or cloth-draped rope hung along the middle of the lists, the enclosure in which the joust was held. It gave direction to the combatants, and the wooden barrier which later replaced the cloth prevented collisions. The knights charged along the tilt in opposite directions, their left or bridle

arms next to the barrier, their lances aimed diagonally across it. The miniature above shows a joust with a barrier. The word tilt was finally applied to the joust itself.

The tournaments and jousts described at length in Arthurian romances not only reflected the chivalric customs of the times in which they were composed; they soon began to influence the conduct of these pastimes in actual life. Some of these events were actually called "Round Tables" after Arthur's famous board. As early as 1223 a French crusading knight held a Round Table at Beirut in Syria in honor of the knighting of his eldest son, and many others are mentioned in the thirteenth and fourteenth centuries. One of these was the joust at Saint-Inglevert, near Calais, in 1390, shown above. In this joust, which took place during a truce in the Hundred Years' War, three French knights challenged all comers, English or otherwise, to fight "a Table Round" over a period of thirty days, in fulfillment of a promise to the ladies of Montpellier. Each knight hung two shields on a great tree before his tent, one signifying combat with sharp and one with blunted lances. Those accepting the challenge chose their weapons by striking the appropriate shield. In the miniature the shields, blazoned with hearts, are hung upon the challengers'

rose-colored pavilions—white hearts on a blue ground, gold hearts on green, and red hearts on gold. The red hearts on gold are repeated on the shield of the French knight in the foreground, and a white veil, probably a lady's favor, floats from his helmet. The joust is pictured in the fashion of the second half of the fifteenth century rather than in that of 1390.

The differences between a Round Table and an ordinary joust or tournament are not clear. Those holding a Round Table evidently kept open house for all comers, providing both fighting and feasting. Perhaps some of the feasts were held at actual round tables like that preserved at Winchester. At some Round Tables knights masqueraded as characters from Arthurian romance, bearing their names and their traditional heraldic arms. Some of the Round Table tournaments came close to drama. A description of one said to have been held by Edward I of England in the late thirteenth century

The heraldic arms of Arthur and fifteen knights of the Round Table. Illuminated page from a French tournament book, about 1470. In the Hofer collection, Harvard College Library

strongly suggests a theatrical performance with assigned parts. "According to custom," says the author, "a play or game was made of King Arthur." The best knights were named after those of the Round Table and were naturally victorious—all except Kay. This unlucky knight was set upon by twenty young men; his saddle girths were cut and he was hurled to the ground. He was not seriously hurt, however, and all the spectators laughed lustily to see him fulfilling his traditional role as a comic character. The king then declared that everything had happened as in Arthur's time and invited those who had borne Arthurian names to share his table at the feast. This account was not written until about fifty years after the tournament was supposed to have taken place, but it probably gives a general idea of such a Round Table. Evidently it was the custom to proclaim at such events that the tournament was held according to the rules of Arthur's court. René, Duke of Anjou, made the same claim for the Round Table which he held in 1446 on the plain near Saumur, where he built a

wooden castle for the occasion outside the city and called it Joyous Gard after Lancelot's dwelling.

The Arthurian arms borne at these Round Tables had been worked out from descriptions in the romances or from imagination, and were well known in armorials and books of tournament rules. A page from such a book is shown here. It is one of several pages giving the arms of Arthurian knights and a description of Arthur and the Round Table, added by an unknown author to a manuscript of the tournament book of René of Anjou. The arms, reading from left to right, are those of Galahad: a field of silver (argent) with a cross in red (gules); Perceval: purple, sprinkled (semé) with crosses of gold (or); Lancelot: silver, with three red bends (diagonal bands drawn in the direction shown); Bors: ermine, with three red bends; Arthur: azure, with thirteen golden crowns; Gawain: purple, with a double-headed golden eagle with wings expanded (displayed); Tristan: green (vert), with a golden lion rampant, its claws and tongue in red; Lionel: silver, sprinkled with six-pointed mullets in black (sable) and bearing three red bends; Helyas: silver, with three red bends and a black horizontal ribbon (label) with three points; Baudemagus: red, with three left-hand gloves in silver; Ydier: red, with three golden lions' heads, their tongues shown in black; Rions: gold, with a purple lion in the position known as passant-guardant, its claws and tongue azure; Carados: azure, with a silver crown; King of Clare: gold, with a cross potent (four small crosses in the angles make this the Jerusalem cross); Duke of Clarence: azure, with a citadel or town in gold, the masonry shown in black; Ector de Maris: silver, sprinkled with black crescents, three red bends, and over all an azure sun.

Tournaments and Round Tables were not confined to kings and nobles. The burghers, who were not permitted to share in the knightly sports, often organized their own. One noteworthy burghers' Round Table was held in 1331 by thirty-one citizens of Tournai, who organized a Society of the Round Table, assumed the names and heraldic arms of Arthurian characters, and invited other cities to a tournament. Fourteen accepted, among them Paris, Bruges, and Amiens. When all had assembled at Tournai, there was a procession of combatants, followed by jousts in the market square and a banquet at the town hall to end the celebration.

The scene opposite suggests a spectacle at some burghers' tournament, although it illustrates a tournament at Arthur's court. The setting here resembles that of a theatrical performance in a town square, surrounded by wooden galleries such as were erected for the more important spectators at the mystery plays performed by the guilds. The aged Arthur in the central gallery, the spectators, and the combatants themselves resemble solid Flemish citizens rather than figures of romance. The artist has transformed the sport of chivalry into an entertainment for such citizens.

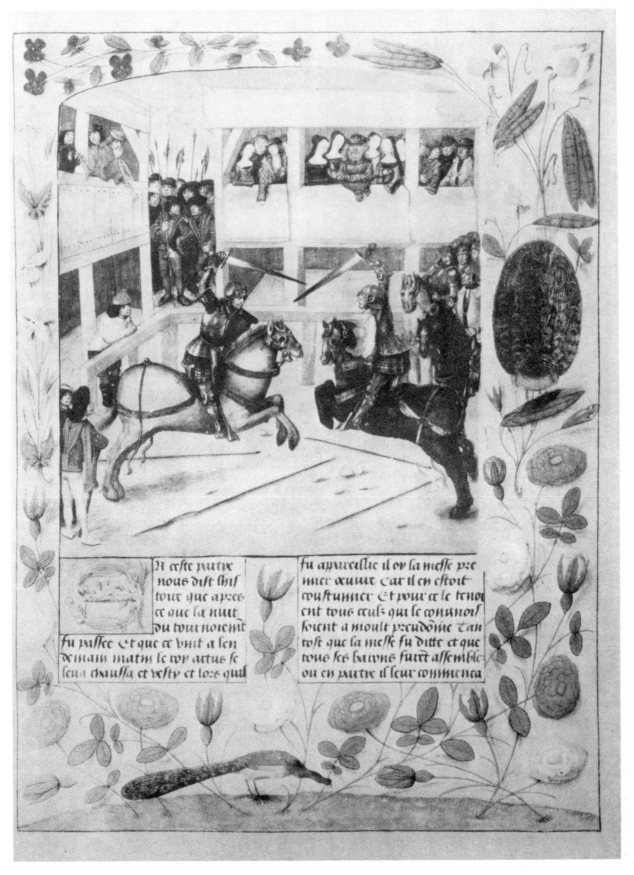

A tournament before Arthur. Manuscript illumination,
Flemish, about 1480-1500, from a French prose romance.
In the Bodleian Library, Oxford, MS Douce, 383

Arthur and Godfrey of Bouillon. Detail of an early XVI century Flemish tapestry. In the Metropolitan Museum

Most of the important representations of Arthur in mediaeval art show him as one of the Nine Worthies. This favorite list of kings and warriors appeared in literature for the first time in 1310, in the *Vows of the Peacock*, a French poem composed by the jongleur Jacques de Longuyon. The nine he named were Hector of Troy, Alexander the Great, and Julius Caesar; Joshua, David, and Judas Maccabaeus; Arthur, Charlemagne, and the crusader Godfrey of Bouillon. Jacques de Longuyon says of Arthur: "I know three Christians such that no man alive ever saw one better than they wearing a bright helm. The fame of Arthur, who ruled Britain, witnesses that he slew Ritho . . . , a giant, in open field, who was so strong, proud, and orgulous that he made a robe of the beards of kings, which kings were held in obedience to him by force. He desired the beard of Arthur, but in that he failed. Arthur slew also on Mont S. Michel a giant so huge that all the folk of the land marveled thereat. In many other places, if the history lie

not, this King Arthur vanquished many a haughty prince."

William Caxton recalled the fame of these Worthies in the preface to his edition of Malory's *Morte d'Arthur* in 1485: "It is notoriously known through the universal world that there be nine worthy and the best that ever were. That is to wit three paynims, three Jews, and three Christian men. As for the paynims they were tofore the Incarnation of Christ, which were named, the first Hector of Troy, of whom the history is come both in ballad and in prose; the second Alexander the Great and the third Julius Caesar, Emperor of Rome, of whom the histories be well-known and had. And as for the three Jews which also were tofore the Incarnation of our Lord, of whom the first was Duke Joshua which brought the children of Israel into the land of behest; the second David, King of Jerusalem; and the third Judas Maccabaeus: of these three the Bible rehearseth all their noble histories and acts. And sith the said Incarnation have been three noble Christian men stalled and admitted through the universal world into the number of the nine best and worthy, of whom was first the noble Arthur, whose noble acts I purpose to write in this present book here following. The second was Charlemagne or Charles the Great, of whom the history is had in many places both in French and English; and the third and last was Godfrey of Bouillon."

Classified lists were very popular in the Middle Ages, and the Nine Worthies became favorites quickly. As early as 1336 they appeared in a pageant at Arras, bearing the heraldic emblems by which they were known. Arthur's traditional device was three crowns, representing England, Scotland, and Brittany, although the number of crowns sometimes varied; the oldest accounts, however, said that he bore either a cross or an image of the Virgin and Child on his shield.

The Museum's large King Arthur tapestry is from a set of the Worthies. In the central part, shown opposite, the king is enthroned in a canopied niche and surrounded by clergy and courtiers on a smaller scale. The figure of the king has a simplicity and strength suggesting the Gothic statues often set beneath such architectural canopies. This hanging, woven in the late fourteenth century, is the earliest surviving tapestry of Arthur and the only one in which he is shown life size. The king's robe is blue with three golden crowns, his mantle soft red lined with the yellow-buff which is used for the architectural framework.

Arthur appears above in a compartment of the Museum's early sixteenth-century tapestry showing scenes from the life of Charlemagne. Godfrey of Bouillon, recognizable by the cross of Jerusalem upon his shield, is looking over Arthur's shoulder. On the blue ground of the king's shield are the three gold crowns, and his robe is soft red lined with ivory white. Godfrey's robe and hat are pale green.

King Arthur. Central part of a tapestry belonging to a
set of the Nine Worthies. French, late XIV century. In
the Metropolitan Museum

Seven of the Worthies. Left to right: Julius Caesar, Joshua, David, Judas Maccabaeus, King Arthur, Charlemagne, Godfrey of Bouillon. Wall painting, about 1430, in the castle of La Manta in northern Italy

Above are seven of the Worthies, painted about 1430 at the North Italian castle of La Manta. The paintings have the decorative effect of tapestries. Fantastically costumed, the heroes stand in a flowery meadow, their shields, bearing their familiar devices, hanging on the trees which break the space into compartments canopied by branches. Below are stanzas in French describing the heroes' exploits. Arthur, with his three crowns, is fifth from the left. His description reads: "I was king of Britain, Scotland, and England. Five hundred kings I conquered, who held their lands from me. I have slain seven great giants in the midst of their land. I went to conquer still another on Mont S. Michel. I saw the Holy Grail. Then Modred made war on me, who slew me five hundred years after God came to earth." At the left is the last of the three pagan heroes, Julius Caesar. Then come Joshua, David, and Judas Maccabaeus; Arthur, Charlemagne, and Godfrey with his Jerusalem cross.

Two statues of Arthur, made three centuries apart, are shown opposite. They illustrate the changes in the king's appearance caused by the fact that artists usually represented heroes in the most up-to-date fashion of the day. The statue of Arthur at Cologne belongs to one of the earliest groups of the Nine Worthies in art and was probably carved about 1325. Arthur's garb in this statue is not widely different from that in which the first romance writers imagined him—complete chain armor, with a long surcoat. His hand is raised to lift the visor of his helmet in the gesture which was the forerunner of the salute.

Between this simple Gothic figure and the elaborately decorated bronze from the workshop of Peter Vischer of Nuremberg lies the change from the Middle Ages to the Renaissance. The second figure was commissioned by Maximilian of Austria, "last of the knights," an admirer of romances and the trappings of chivalry. He directed that Arthur, with several other Worthies, be represented among the statues of his ancestors on his monument at Innsbruck. This figure shows Arthur in the elaborately embossed parade armor of the early sixteenth century. His shield, which was made a few years later than the statue, bears, not the familiar three crowns, but the lilies and lions of England, as if to suggest an actual English king rather than a hero of romance. Indeed, the emperor probably included Arthur in this group partly because of a fancied claim to the English crown. In return for supporting Perkin Warbeck, the pretender to the English throne who declared himself one of the little princes imprisoned by Richard III in the Tower of London, Maximilian had been promised the succession to the English throne should Warbeck die without children.

LEFT: *Statue of King Arthur, about 1325. In the Hall of the Hanseatic League, Rathaus, Cologne.* RIGHT: *Bronze statue of King Arthur, 1513. Workshop of Peter Vischer the Elder. In the Court Chapel, Innsbruck*

Arthur in Avalon. Illustration by Dante Gabriel Rossetti for an edition of Tennyson's poems published by Edward Moxon, London, 1857

When the stories of Arthur were revived in the nineteenth century, after being long out of fashion, the fairyland of Avalon delighted poets and artists as much as it had in the Middle Ages. Rossetti's woodcut, above, illustrates Tennyson's early poem *The Palace of Art*, first published in 1832. On the walls of this imaginary palace were painted scenes from nature, legend, and romance. Among these

> mythic Uther's deeply-wounded son
> In some fair space of sloping greens
> Lay, dozing in the vale of Avalon,
> And watch'd by weeping queens.

The sorrowing queens almost hide the bearded head of Arthur at the left, and in the background the ship which brought the king from his last battlefield rides close above them. The sharply tilted perspective and the absence of any visible horizon suggest a remote and hidden place, far from the world of time—the realm of fairyland. This woodcut of Rossetti's and others in the same volume, as well as many of his early drawings and water colors, are filled with the sense of wonder and mystery with which the nineteenth century liked to clothe the Middle Ages.

In his *Morte d'Arthur*, published in 1842, Tennyson took up the story of Arthur's voyage to Avalon, which was not mentioned in *The Palace of Art*. although Rossetti suggested it by the ship in the background. Later the poet expanded the *Morte d'Arthur*, renamed it *The Passing of Arthur*, and used it to close his series of *Idylls of the King*. The description of this voyage in *The Passing of Arthur* is based closely on the last chapters of Malory, with changes and additions which reflect the differences in thought between the fifteenth and the nineteenth century. Arthur and Bedivere, waiting by "the level lake" in "the long glories of the winter moon," saw

> how there hove a dusky barge,
> Dark as a funeral scarf from stem to stern,
> Beneath them; and descending they were ware
> That all the decks were dense with stately forms,
> Black-stoled, black-hooded, like a dream—by these
> Three queens with crowns of gold—and from them rose
> A cry that shiver'd to the tingling stars.

> . . . .

> Then murmur'd Arthur, "Place me in the barge,"
> So to the barge they came. There those three queens
> Put forth their hands, and took the King, and wept.
> But she that rose the tallest of them all
> And fairest laid his head upon her lap,
> And loosed the shatter'd casque, and chafed his hands,
> And call'd him by his name, complaining loud.

So far Tennyson followed Malory's story closely, though adding and expanding descriptions. But he changed Bedivere's farewell from the simple, personal question, "What shall become of me?" to a generalized expression of the doubt and loneliness of men who see the end of stable and familiar things:

> Then loudly cried the bold Sir Bedivere:
> "Ah! my Lord Arthur, whither shall I go?
> Where shall I hide my forehead and my eyes?
> For now I see the true old times are dead,
> When every morning brought a noble chance,
> And every chance brought out a noble knight.

> . . . .

> But now the whole Round Table is dissolved
> Which was an image of the mighty world;
> And I, the last, go forth companionless,
> And the days darken round me, and the years,
> Among new men, strange faces, other minds."

In Malory, Arthur's reply also was direct and personal: "Comfort thyself, . . . and do as well as thou mayest, for in me is no trust for to trust in; for I will into the vale of Avilion to heal me of my grievous wound: and if thou hear never more of me, pray for my soul." Malory's brief words carry a bare sense of human loneliness in the face of death. But he lived when Christian certainties were still comparatively unshaken and his audience had enough faith in the teachings of the Church to accept its consolation. Tennyson, in an age of widespread doubt, treated Arthur's story not only as a narrative but also as an allegory "shadowing Sense at war with Soul." So he expanded Arthur's farewell into a universal answer to the questions of his time, combining the scientific idea of progress through change with a hope based upon religious faith:

> "The old order changeth, yielding place to new,
> And God fulfils himself in many ways,
> Lest one good custom should corrupt the world.
> Comfort thyself; what comfort is in me?
> I have lived my life, and that which I have done
> May He within himself make pure! but thou,

If thou shouldst never see my face again,
Pray for my soul. More things are wrought by prayer
Than this world dreams of. Wherefore, let thy voice
Rise like a fountain for me night and day.
For what are men better than sheep or goats
That nourish a blind life within the brain,
If, knowing God, they lift not hands of prayer
Both for themselves and those who call them friend?
For so the whole round earth is every way
Bound by gold chains about the feet of God.
But now farewell. I am going a long way
With these thou seest—if indeed I go—
For all my mind is clouded with a doubt—
To the island-valley of Avilion;
Where falls not hail, or rain, or any snow,
Nor ever wind blows loudly; but it lies
Deep-meadow'd, happy, fair with orchard lawns
And bowery hollows crown'd with summer sea,
Where I will heal me of my grievous wound."

Malory told impartially of Arthur's burial and of the belief that he was "not dead, but had by the will of our Lord Jesu into another place." Tennyson's Bedivere, though remembering the prophecy that Arthur shall return, is shaken by the doubts which clouded the poet's time:

"He passes to be king among the dead,
And after healing of his grievous wound
He comes again; but—if he come no more—"

Edward Burne-Jones's Arthur in Avalon, above, gives a different presentation from that in Rossetti's woodcut. Burne-Jones has gone deeper than Rossetti into the heart of fairyland. The queens no longer lament so passionately, but keep vigil in a quiet place, "Where falls not hail, or rain, or any snow," until the king shall awake and return to mortal lands. Arthur, "king that was and king that shall be," lies asleep under a canopy of beaten gold. Two queens sit by him sorrowing, one at his head, one at his feet, and a third stands behind him bearing the

Arthur in Avalon. Unfinished painting by Edward Burne-Jones, begun in 1881. In the collection of Sidney Goldmann, England

crown of the future. The crown of the past lies upon the grass. Four maidens play soft music, while others wait with half-raised trumpets to herald the king's awakening, and watchers look beyond the battlements of fairyland. The foreground is filled with iris, columbines, and forget-me-nots, painted with loving care.

In his early years Burne-Jones was strongly influenced by Rossetti, but he soon developed the distinct personal style shown in this picture. The figures are grouped almost in one plane, their proportions are exaggeratedly tall and slender, and their faces are marked by a dreamy wistfulness. Details are painted with exquisite fidelity. A comment made by the artist while at work on the picture shows clearly that his flat, tapestrylike composition was based on considered principles. Having rubbed out one of the watchers, who had been placed so far back that she had to be shown much smaller than the rest, he said: "We have lost one thing in the world which we need never expect to get back again, and that is the right to put a figure in the background of the same size as those in the front. The Greeks did it, and the old Italians, and it used to be quite right, but we can't any longer. We have eaten of the fruit of the tree of knowledge and can't have our garden of Eden any more."

The story of Merlin and Nimue was a favorite with Burne-Jones. In 1857 he tried his hand at painting it in the debating hall of the Oxford Union, but never finished the fresco. The two pictures following show different versions of the enchanter's doom as well as the artist's early and more fully developed styles. In 1861, while still under Rossetti's influence, he painted the water color

Merlin and Nimue. Water color by Edward Burne-Jones, 1861. In the Victoria and Albert Museum

Merlin and Nimue, above. It was based directly upon Malory's description, part of which is quoted on the frame. Burne-Jones has shown the stone under which Merlin was imprisoned as a gravestone that is raising itself by enchantment, while a weird bluish light glows from beneath. Nimue reads the fatal spell from Merlin's own book of magic as she leads him toward the opening grave. Behind him lies a dark lake reflecting the pale sky, and beyond the lake rise blue and jagged hills.

In The Beguiling of Merlin, opposite, Burne-Jones turned from Malory's version to that of the earlier romances. When the picture was exhibited in the Grosvenor Gallery in 1877, the catalogue quoted the following passage from the romance of Merlin:

"It fell on a day that they went through the forest that is called the Forest of Breceliande, and found a bush that was fair and high, of white hawthorn, full of flowers, and there they sat in the shadow. And Merlin fell on sleep; and when she felt that he was on sleep she arose softly and began her enchantments, such as Merlin had taught her, and made the ring nine times and nine times the enchantments. . . .

"And then he looked about him, and him seemed he was in the fairest tower of the world and the most strong; neither of iron was it fashioned, nor steel, nor timber, nor of stone, but of the air without any other thing; and in sooth so strong it is that it may never be undone while the world endureth."

This painting, done in oils between 1872 and 1877, is in the artist's own characteristic style, with tall, slender figures, clinging drapery, and elaborate detail.

Matthew Arnold had used a similar version of Merlin's imprisonment at the end of his *Tristram and Iseult* in 1852. In his poem the beguiling damsel was called Vivian —a name given her in some of the romances, probably because of mistakes in copying Nimue or Ninien. But her reason for imprisoning the magician, according to Arnold, was not love but boredom, as in Malory's story:

> They sate them down together, and a sleep
> Fell upon Merlin, more like death, so deep.
> Her finger on her lips, then Vivian rose,
> And from her brown-locked head the wimple throws,
> And takes it in her hand, and waves it over
> The blossomed thorn-tree, and her sleeping lover.
> Nine times she waved the fluttering wimple round,
> And made a little plot of magic ground.
> And in that daisied circle, as men say,
> Is Merlin prisoner till the judgment-day;
> But she herself whither she will can rove—
> For she was passing weary of his love.

Tennyson's *Merlin and Vivien*, published in 1859, followed the same version but changed the hawthorn to an oak and made Vivien actively malicious, instead of merely tired of Merlin's attentions. She is a symbol of the power of evil against which the Round Table fights, and she wishes to destroy Merlin's usefulness in order to harm the court which has scorned her. In Tennyson's idyll, Vivien followed the magician to Broceliande:

> For Merlin had once told her of a charm,
> The which if any wrought on any one
> With woven paces and with waving arms,
> The man so wrought on ever seem'd to lie
> Closed in the four walls of a hollow tower,
> From which was no escape for evermore;
> And none could find that man for evermore,
> Nor could he see but him who wrought the charm
> Coming and going, and he lay as dead
> And lost to life and use and name and fame.
> And Vivien ever sought to work the charm
> Upon the great enchanter of the time,
> As fancying that her glory would be great
> According to his greatness whom she quench'd.
>
> . . . .
>
> And in the wild woods of Broceliande,
> Before an oak, so hollow, huge, and old
> It look'd a tower of ivied masonwork,
> At Merlin's feet the wily Vivien lay,"

begging that she might learn the charm. At last Merlin

> yielded, told her all the charm, and slept.
> Then, in one moment, she put forth the charm
> Of woven paces and of waving hands,
> And in the hollow oak he lay as dead,
> And lost to life and use and name and fame.

The Beguiling of Merlin. Painting by Edward Burne-Jones,
1872-1877. Lady Lever Gallery, Port Sunlight, England.

The finding of Excalibur. Detail of a stained-glass window by Charles J. Connick, installed in the Princeton University chapel in 1931

Among the windows of the Princeton University chapel is one devoted to the history of Arthur as told by Malory. It belongs to a group of four designed and made by Charles J. Connick to illustrate great epics of the Christian world, the others being Dante's *Divine Comedy*, Milton's *Paradise Lost* and *Paradise Regained*, treated as one, and Bunyan's *Pilgrim's Progress*. The lower section of the Arthur window, which was installed in 1931, is illustrated opposite. Its dominant colors are blue, red, and silvery white. The complete window soars, tall and slender, into the delicate tracery at its top, its groups of small panels alternating with rows of tall, single figures. The composition of the panels is at once restful and vigorous, with closing curves and bold diagonals.

The finding of the sword Excalibur is a panel at the right side of the lower section. As Malory tells the story, Arthur's sword had broken in battle, and he told Merlin of his plight. "No force, said Merlin, hereby is a sword that shall be yours, an I may. So they rode till they came to a lake, the which was a fair water and broad, and in the midst of the lake Arthur was ware of an arm clothed in white samite, that held a fair sword in that hand. Lo said Merlin, yonder is that sword that I spake of. With that they saw a damosel going upon the lake. What damosel is that? said Arthur. That is the Lady of the Lake, said Merlin; and within that lake is a rock, and therein is as fair a place as any on earth, and richly beseen; and this damosel will come to you anon, and then speak ye fair to her that she will give you that sword. Anon withal came the damosel unto Arthur, and saluted him, and he her again. Damosel, said Arthur, what sword is that, that yonder the arm holdeth above the water? I would it were mine, for I have no sword. Sir Arthur, king, said the damosel, that sword is mine, and if ye will give me a gift when I ask it you, ye shall have it. By my faith, said Arthur, I will give you what gift ye will ask. Well! said the damosel, go ye into yonder barge, and row yourself to the sword, and take it and the scabbard with you, and I will ask my gift when I see my time. So Sir Arthur and Merlin alit and tied their horses to two trees, and so they went into the ship, and when they came to the sword that the hand held, Sir Arthur took it up by the handles, and took it with him, and the arm and the hand went under the water." In another passage Malory said of Excalibur that "it gave light like thirty torches." In the window panel Merlin rows the barge while Arthur stands solemnly erect, with bowed head, holding out his hands for the sword, whose brilliance is suggested by a jagged, flamelike band. The diagonal band which crosses the panel bears the inscription "How Arthur gate Excalybur."

In the section of the window shown opposite, the first scene represents Malory writing his book behind prison bars. Next appears the child Arthur, in the arms of Merlin, who keeps watch over his upbringing. Then come the acknowledgment of Arthur as king and the winning of Excalibur, followed by the king's wedding with Guenevere in a little chapel, with the tall figure of Merlin in the foreground warning in vain that this marriage will bring woe. Next Arthur fights with Sir Accolon of Gaul, to whom Morgan Le Fay had given the true Excalibur, deceiving the king with a false blade which broke in his hand. Only by the power of the Lady of the Lake did Arthur regain his true sword and conquer Accolon. After this comes the king's last battle, with the traitor Mordred, and finally his passing to Avalon. In the upper left of this scene, the arm rising from the lake takes Excalibur again beneath the water. The scenes are crowned by four tall figures. Arthur and Mordred face each other in the center. The Lady of the Lake, holding the true Excalibur, is at the right, beside Arthur. Morgan le Fay, with the false sword, stands beside Mordred at the left. This section of the window, Mr. Connick has noted, is devoted to the elements of violence and magic in the legend of Arthur. The section above it shows scenes of chivalry, and the top panels emphasize the religious theme in the story of the Grail.

The history of King Arthur. Lower section of a stained-glass window by Charles J. Connick, installed in the Princeton University chapel in 1931. The designs for this window, including the panel shown opposite, are based on Malory's "Morte d'Arthur"

Printed illustrations have undoubtedly done more than any other form of art to shape the nineteenth- and twentieth-century idea of Arthur and his court. One of the first outstanding nineteenth-century books with illustrations of Arthurian stories was the volume of Tennyson's poems published by Edward Moxon of London in 1857. It had wood engravings by Rossetti, Holman Hunt, Millais, Daniel Maclise, and other English artists. Some of these illustrations have great beauty, while others are mediocre; many of them have been widely reprinted in the United States in the popular Household Editions of Tennyson. Two of the best known of these woodcuts, the Finding of Excalibur and the Passing of Arthur, by Maclise, are shown opposite. Since 1857 such widely different illustrators as Aubrey Beardsley, Gustave Doré, Howard Pyle, Arthur Rackham, Edmund Dulac, and Harold Foster have carried on the interpretations of Arthurian stories and characters.

Newspapers have spread some of these interpretations widely. Edmund Dulac's pictures of *Seven Tales from King Arthur's Court*, for instance, published with texts by John Erskine in the *American Weekly* during 1940, reached a circulation of over seven million. The Tale of Arthur's Sword, Excalibur, above, is from this series. As in Malory the damsel is "going upon the lake" and Merlin is with Arthur in the boat; Maclise's illustration of the scene, opposite, follows Tennyson's version in which the king rows out alone to get the sword. Harold Foster's weekly comic series, *Prince Valiant in the Days of King Arthur*, has been widely syndicated since its beginning in 1936. This new hero shares some of his adventures with Tristan, Gawain, and Lancelot, although he often roam far afield.

The illustration by Doré at the right suggests the elfin charm which lingered about the story of Arthur in the nineteenth century. It was the inspiration, too, of the airy second movement of Edward MacDowell's Sonata Eroica, which bears the motto: *Flos regum Arthurus*—"Arthur, Flower of Kings." MacDowell wrote of this Arthurian sonata, published in 1895: "While not exactly programme music I had in mind the Arthurian legend when writing this work. The first movement [marked in the score 'Slow, with nobility'] typifies the coming of Arthur. The Scherzo [the second movement, 'Elf-like, as light and swift as possible'] was suggested by a picture of Doré showing a knight in the woods surrounded by elves. The third movement ['Tenderly, longingly, yet with passion'] was suggested by my idea of Guenevere, and the last movement ['Fiercely, very fast'] represents the passing of Arthur." The "picture of Doré" illustrates a passage in Tennyson's *Guinevere* in which a little maid at the nunnery to which the queen has fled describes the fairy life of Britain in her father's time, when Arthur and the Round Table alike were young and full of hope. Her father, riding through the woods,

Himself beheld three spirits mad with joy
Come dashing down on a tall wayside flower,
That shook beneath them as the thistle shakes
When three gray linnets wrangle for the seed.
And still at evenings on before his horse
The flickering fairy-circle wheel'd and broke
Flying, and link'd again, and wheel'd and broke
Flying, and all the land was full of life.

TRISTAN AND ISEULT

Tristan's name comes from that of an actual person, Drust, king of the Picts of Scotland about A.D. 780, and some of his adventures belong to this king's saga. The Celts of Wales, Cornwall, and Brittany changed the hero's name to Drystan or Trystan and made him the nephew of King Mark of Cornwall. At first the stories of Tristan and Arthur had no connection, but the Welsh brought them together and most of the French romances made Tristan a knight of the Round Table.

The story of Tristan and Iseult, marked from the beginning as a theme for tragedy, was told most beautifully by the romancers of the twelfth and early thirteenth centuries. Among the twelfth-century French poets who wrote of Tristan was the Anglo-Norman Thomas of Britain, whose romance was the source of one of the most beautiful of Tristan stories—Gottfried von Strassburg's unfinished poem, written in German about 1210. Malory's tale of the lovers was taken from a later prose version, which had lost much of the beauty and freshness of the earlier poems.

Although love is the central theme, Tristan's adven-

tures bulk large as well. As a young orphan he came to his uncle's castle at Tintagel on the Cornish coast and was recognized as heir by the unmarried king. At this time Cornwall was forced to send to Ireland a yearly tribute of noble youths unless a Cornish champion could overcome the Irish king's brother-in-law, Morolt, who came to collect the tribute. Tristan defeated him, leaving a piece of his sword in Morolt's skull. Morolt was borne to his sister, Iseult, the Irish queen, who was the most skillful healer in the world, but she could not save him. Her daughter, Iseult the Fair, kept the fragment of the sword and vowed vengeance upon the slayer. But Morolt's poisoned sword had wounded Tristan, and he knew that only the Irish queen could heal him. So, disguised as a minstrel, he sailed to Ireland. There the queen healed him, asking only that he teach her daughter Iseult the arts of music.

When Tristan returned to Cornwall, the Cornish lords were urging Mark to marry. The king refused for a long time, but finally agreed to ask the hand of the Princess Iseult, of whose beauty and wisdom Tristan had told him. The jealous knights urged Tristan to undertake the embassy to Ireland, hoping that he would be

LEFT: *Tristan voyaging to Ireland to ask the hand of Iseult for King Mark*

ABOVE: *Tristan cutting out the dragon's tongue; the seneschal fleeing. Wall paintings, about 1400, in the Summer House of Castle Runkelstein*

killed, and were far from happy when they were commanded to accompany him.

Ireland was then ravaged by a fierce dragon and the king had promised the Princess Iseult to the man who should kill it, so Tristan made his plans accordingly. The sight of the Irish court seneschal and several other knights fleeing guided him to the dragon's lair, and he attacked the monster. After a hard fight he killed the dragon and cut out its tongue, which he placed in his bosom. Then he staggered toward a stream and fell unconscious.

Meanwhile the seneschal returned, found the dragon, and cut off its head. Then he went to the court to claim the princess. The two Iseults were certain that he had not killed the beast, and they set out by night, with the princess's handmaid and friend, Brangoene, to learn the truth. They found Tristan unconscious, disarmed him, and discovered the tongue. Realizing that he was the slayer of the dragon they carried him secretly to the palace. There the Princess Iseult looked at his sword, found the notch in it, and fitted into it the fragment from Morolt's skull. In her rage she would have slain the defenseless knight, but her mother and Brangoene re-

strained her, and finally both Iseults, and the Irish king as well, forgave Tristan, realizing that "a man defends his life as best he may." When the seneschal returned for the princess, bringing the head as proof, Tristan bade the court look for the dragon's tongue. When no tongue was found Tristan produced it, and all agreed that he was the slayer. So Tristan won Iseult's hand for Mark.

Tristan's voyage to Ireland to bring Iseult to Mark and his cutting out the dragon's tongue are among the scenes from the story painted in the late fourteenth century at Castle Runkelstein in Tyrol. The scenes, in grayish green monochrome with touches of scarlet where blood appears, form a band of continuous narrative around the walls of a room, but are separated from one another by rocks. Between 1503 and 1511 the Emperor Maximilian, who then owned the castle, commissioned

41

three court painters to restore the decorations "on account of the good old History," with the result that sixteenth-century costumes, plumes, and armor were laid over a fourteenth-century composition.

Iseult's mother had entrusted to Brangoene a drink for Mark and Iseult on their wedding night, "a love potion of such power and magic that did any two drink thereof they must needs, without will of their own, love each other above all things from that day forward," says Gottfried von Strassburg. One day as Tristan and Iseult sat together on the ship Tristan was thirsty, and a little maid, in Brangoene's absence, brought what she thought was a flask of wine, but which was the magic potion. Iseult drank first and after her Tristan. And then "but one heart had they—her grief was his sadness, his sadness her grief." When Brangoene found the empty flask and saw the lovers grow pale and wan, she told them what fate had overtaken them. Iseult had no thought "save of Love and Tristan," but he, trained in feudal loyalty, "knew well that he owed both faith and honour to Mark, who had sent him to fetch his bride, and the twain fought hard with his love, and vexed heart and soul between them, yet was it of no avail, for since he had chosen Love, Honour and Faith alike must needs be put to the worse." Gottfried thus laid upon the lovers some burden of responsibility, despite his use of the potion which represented fate.

So the ship came to Cornwall, and there Mark married Iseult, but her heart belonged to Tristan alone. They met so often that the court of Cornwall became suspicious. Then, counseled by Brangoene, Tristan cut twigs from an olive tree which grew by a fountain in the orchard, carved on them the letters T and I, and threw them into the little stream that ran from this spring past Iseult's chamber, as a sign that he would be waiting for her by the fountain. Thus they met secretly many times,

but at last Melot, Mark's dwarf, saw them and led Mark to the orchard, where the king hid himself in the branches of the olive tree. But when the lovers met, the bright moonlight cast Mark's reflection into the fountain. Tristan and Iseult saw it and talked so discreetly that the king's jealousy was quieted for a time.

This tryst at the fountain was a favorite subject in mediaeval art. It was painted on castle walls, carved on ivory mirror backs and caskets, used in embroideries and enamels, and even carved on the capitals and choir stalls of churches. On the ivory casket above, the king parts the branches of the tree to peer down, while his reflection shows, like a severed head, in the water gushing from the fountain. Tristan, falcon on wrist, points out the reflection to Iseult, who raises one hand in a gesture of polite conversation, while she strokes her lapdog with the other. The unicorn laying his head in a maiden's lap while a hunter strikes him has no connection with the story.

In the scene of Tristan and Iseult at the fountain on the walls of Castle Rhäzüns, Tristan stands at the left and Iseult at the right, attended by Brangoene, who holds a garland of roses. The faithful handmaid is shown much smaller than Iseult to indicate the difference in rank. Between Tristan and Iseult is a pine tree in which Mark is hidden; his head looks out from its feathery branches like a crowned sun. The names of the lovers and the king are painted beside them. Beneath the tree stand a unicorn and a deer, and birds and night moths flutter about. The scene is closed at the ends by the arms of the Rhäzüns family.

Most beautiful of all the remaining scenes of the fountain tryst is that at the castle of Saint-Floret, illustrated on pages 44 and 45; the tryst at Runkelstein was destroyed by the fall of a wall in 1868. At Saint-Floret, Tristan is painted on the left jamb of a deep-set window and Iseult on the right. Mark's head is in the arch above the window and below was once the fountain, now destroyed by weathering. Below the figures is the crenelated orchard wall. The lovers are shown with a majestic largeness of scale and simplicity, and they bear themselves with an air of stately wistfulness and restraint which is as close as mediaeval romance painting came to the passionate emotion of the story. Other half-ruined scenes in the same room show Tristan in battle.

Mark's suspicions, set at rest for a time, awoke again,

Tristan and Iseult at the fountain. Wall painting in Castle Rhäzüns, Switzerland

and he banished Tristan and Iseult from court. They departed, attended by one faithful squire, to a cavern, "round, large, and lofty," deep in the Forest of Morrois. Gottfried von Strassburg's description of this forest and the lovers' life there is one of the most exquisite descriptions of natural beauty in mediaeval literature.

"All around the hill and towards the valley were countless trees, whose boughs and foliage gave a fair shade. On one side was a little glade and a spring of water, cool and fresh and clear as sunlight, and above the spring were again three lindens, which sheltered it alike from sun and rain; and all over the glade the bright blossoms and green grass strove with each other for the mastery.... Nor did it vex them that they were thus alone in the wild woodland; what should they want with other company? Even good King Arthur never held at his court a feast that might have brought them greater joy and refreshment.... They had a court, they had a council, which brought them naught but joy. Their courtiers were the green trees, the shade and the sunlight, the streamlet and the spring; flowers, grass, leaf and blossom, which refreshed their eyes. Their service was the song of the birds, the little brown nightingales, the throstles, and the merles; and other wood birds.... Their love was their high feast, which brought them a thousand times daily the joy of Arthur's Round Table and the

fellowship of his knights." But after a while Mark's heart changed again and he recalled them from their exile.

Glimpses of the lovers' life in the Forest of Morrois were painted, with other scenes from romance, on the beams of a ceiling of the Chiaramonte Palace in Palermo between 1377 and 1380. A detail of one of these paintings is shown on page 46. The lovers ride into the forest followed by the faithful squire, who appears again holding the two horses while Tristan and Iseult enjoy a picnic spread upon a rock. They have evidently brought with them the conveniences of civilization, for the food is set out upon a fringed napkin and there are dishes and knives. Iseult's costume, trailing and closely fitted, with long, tight sleeves and hanging oversleeves, is of a style much better adapted to a court than a forest. The figures have a dainty, childlike grace which harmonizes well with this idyllic interlude.

After the lovers had returned to the court of Cornwall, the king found them in each others' arms. He departed to call his council to sentence them to death, and the two knew that the end had come. "Heart's lady, fair Iseult, said Tristan, now must we part.... Sweet love, fair Iseult, kiss me, and bid me farewell!

43

King Mark

Tristan and Iseult at the fountain; King Mark watching from a tree. Wall painting, about 1350, in the castle of Saint-Floret in Auvergne. Tristan, in white and red, points toward Mark. Iseult, who wears a blue-green gown with violet sleeves and a white gorget about her throat and chin, repeats his gesture with her exaggeratedly long and slender fingers. Tristan's figure is painted on the left jamb of a recessed window, Iseult's on the right, and the king's head is in the arch above

Tristan

Iseult

Tristan and Iseult in the Forest of Morrois. Detail of a painted ceiling beam, 1377-1380. In the Chiaramonte Palace, Palermo

---

"She stepped a little back, and spake, sighing: Our hearts and our souls have been too long and too closely knit together that they may ever learn forgetfulness. . . . We two have loved and sorrowed in such true fellowship unto this time, we should not find it over-hard to keep the same faith even to death." So Tristan fled to Brittany, and when Mark's council found the queen alone they reproved him for his suspicions.

In Brittany there lived Iseult of the White Hands, whose brother was Tristan's friend. She loved Tristan and he, though he could not forget Iseult of Ireland, was comforted by her affection and the sound of her name. So, when no word had come for a long time from Iseult the Fair, Tristan married the maid of Brittany. Gottfried's poem ends just before their marriage, but other romancers finished the story.

After a time Tristan was wounded with a poisoned spear and he knew that he would die unless Iseult of Ireland, who had her mother's skill, could heal him. So he sent the faithful Kurwenal to Cornwall, to ask her to come to him, saying: "If for love of me she will come, then I pray thee to set a white sail to the ship; but if she cometh not, then let the sail be black, for I shall know she loveth me no more." Iseult of Ireland left straightway with Kurwenal, but before the ship could reach Brittany Tristan had grown too weak to watch for it and had placed Iseult of the White Hands at the window. As the ship drew near, she, who "knew well who it was that Tristan loved," told him that the sails were black. "Then Tristan spake no word, but turned his face to the wall, and said in his heart: God keep thee, my love Iseult, for I shall look on thee no more, and with that he loosed his hold of the life he had held till then, and his soul departed."

Iseult of Ireland heard the bells toll for Tristan's death and went to where he "lay dead on the bier, and beside him sat Iseult of the white hand. Then Iseult of Ireland looked upon her: Why sittest thou here beside the dead, thou who hast slain him? Arise, and get thee hence! And Iseult of the white hand arose and drew aside, for she feared the queen.

"But Iseult of Ireland spake no word more, but laid her down on the bier by her lover, and put her arms around him, and sighed once, and her soul departed from her body."

King Mark pursued Iseult to Brittany and there Kurwenal told him "all that had chanced, and the secret of the love potion. . . . And Mark spake, weeping: Alas! Tristan, hadst thou but trusted in me, and told me all the truth, then had I given Iseult to thee for wife.

"Then he bade them embalm the bodies, and he bare them back with him to Tintagel, and laid them in marble tombs on either side of the chapel wherein the kings of his line lay buried. And by the tomb of Tristan he bade them plant a rose-tree, and by that of Iseult a vine, and the two reached toward each other across the chapel, and wove branches and root so closely together that no man hereafter might separate them."

The miniature opposite shows the beginning and the end of the story in one of those telescoped narrative pictures that were so popular in the Middle Ages. In the foreground, near the coast marked "Ireland," where Iseult's father stands with his court, is the ship bound for Cornwall, with trumpeters in blue and rose sounding a farewell upon golden trumpets. Tristan and Iseult drink the potion, not alone, but surrounded by their retinue like star players among their cast. Above is the shore of Brittany, thick with towers, from which departs another ship, bearing the bodies of the lovers toward Cornwall. Ship and sails and sailors are in black; only the bier where the bodies lie is covered with blue and gold. A taper burns beside it and at the head is Tristan's golden sword. At the left rises the shore of Cornwall with the towers and crags of Tintagel, where the lovers' bodies are to lie in the chapel of the Cornish kings.

The departure of Iseult for Cornwall, the drinking of the love potion, and the return of the lover's bodies to Cornwall. Manuscript illumination, about 1470, from a French prose romance of Tristan. In the Bibliothèque Nationale, Paris, Fr. 103, fol. 1

La Belle Yseult. Pen and ink study by William Morris, about 1857. In the collection of Henry Currie Marillier, England

In the story of Tristan and Iseult the nineteenth century found a theme of passionate and tragic love fitted for infinite variations. It inspired poems by Matthew Arnold, Swinburne, and Tennyson, paintings by Rossetti, Burne-Jones, and William Morris, and Wagner's famous opera. Morris's unfinished drawing of Iseult, at the left, was probably done in 1857, while the artist was working with Rossetti and his friends on the decoration of the debating hall of the Oxford Union with scenes from Malory. His own subject was Sir Palamedes watching Sir Tristram and La Belle Iseult. The drawing is a study for the only painting Morris is known to have finished—a full-length picture of Jane Burden as Iseult in mediaeval costume in a mediaeval chamber, done in 1858 and now in the Tate Gallery. Miss Burden, who married Morris in 1859, also posed for Rossetti's study of Guenevere, illustrated on page 60, which suggests her dark and stately beauty.

In 1857 Swinburne, an undergraduate at Oxford, was introduced to Rossetti, Morris, and Burne-Jones, and the four became close friends. Swinburne listened to Morris's Arthurian poems, which were published the next year, and was fired with enthusiasm for subjects from romance. In December, 1857, he published in *Undergraduate Papers* the first canto of a poem on *Queen Yseult*, showing the influence both of Morris's verse forms and of the subject he was painting. Swinburne's friends assumed that some day he would write a great poem on the story, but this did not appear for many years. No more of the early poem was published at that time, but five additional cantos were discovered in 1918 and printed in 1925.

Rossetti's water color of Tristram and Iseult drinking the love potion had its origin in a design made in 1862, when the artist, with Morris, Burne-Jones, and other friends, was at work on a group of stained-glass panels illustrating Malory's story of the lovers. According to Malory, Tristram and "La Beale Isoud" grew thirsty in the ship's cabin and "saw a little flacket of gold stand by them, and it seemed by the colour and the taste that it was noble wine. Then Sir Tristram took the flacket in his hand, and said, Madam Isoud, here is the best drink that ever ye drank. . . . Then they laughed and made good cheer, and either drank to other freely, and they thought never drink that ever they drank to other was so sweet nor so good. But by that their drink was in their bodies, they loved either other so well that never their love departed for weal neither for woe." In the picture opposite, the god of love floats behind Tristram and flames, suggesting awakening passion, burst from the cups and from the "golden flacket" on the table. Swinburne had suggested the same symbolism in the lines of his early *Queen Yseult*:

But the drink her mother gave
In the carven chalice brave
Like warm gold did float and wave.

Tristram and Yseult Drinking the Love Potion. Water color by Dante Gabriel Rossetti, painted in 1867 after a design for stained glass done in 1862. In the collection of Lady Hood, London, 1939. The stained-glass panels, made for the house of Walter Dunlop by the firm of Morris, Marshall, Faulkner, and Company, are now in the Bradford Municipal Museum; Rossetti's original cartoon is in the Birmingham Museum and Art Gallery

The scene had already been described in one contemporary English poem—Matthew Arnold's *Tristram and Iseult*, first published in 1852. In Arnold's poem, Tristram, waiting on his deathbed for the coming of Iseult, remembers the past in dramatic flashes. He recalls the drinking of the potion and hears Iseult say:

> "Ah! would I were in those green fields at play,
> Not pent on shipboard this delicious day!
> Tristram, I pray thee, of thy courtesy,
> Reach me my golden cup that stands by thee,
> But pledge me in it first for courtesy."

But all Arnold's characters were tempered by the endurance and self-control which were his answer to the problems of life. Unlike the mediaeval Tristan, the hero has been a conscientious husband to Iseult of Brittany and a kindly father to their children. Iseult of Ireland has filled her place as Mark's queen with dignity if not with love, and as she sinks beside Tristram's couch her face has "a tranquil, settled loveliness"—words which could never have been used of the mediaeval Iseult. And Iseult of Brittany, who is the real heroine of the poem, holds no grudge against her rival, though afterwards she tells her children the tale of Merlin and Vivian as an example of what men will do for love. In keeping with nineteenth-century sentiment, Arnold brought Iseult of Ireland to Tristram before his death, as Wagner was to do in his opera five years later. Arnold's poem was based, not on Malory, but on older versions, which he had discovered in a manner characteristic of his intellectual curiosity. He wrote that he had read the story first in "an article in a French review on the romance literature." Later he looked it up in Malory and saw that it was told differently there, but by that time, fortunately, the shape of the poem was set. The article, by Théodore de la Villemarqué in the *Revue de Paris* for 1841, discussed the early French versions, including that of Thomas of Britain.

Tennyson told the end of the lovers' story in his *Last Tournament* in 1872, using the version common to Malory and most of the prose romances, in which Mark killed Tristan in Iseult's presence. Malory had not shown the two at their best, and Tennyson made them still less attractive. He used the story to illustrate the general lowering of the ideals of Arthur's court and the degeneration of character following unlawful passion—a far cry from the twelfth-century praise of courtly love.

Meanwhile Swinburne had been keeping in mind the poem on this story which his friends had long expected, and in 1882 he published his *Tristram of Lyonesse*. He had never approved of Tennyson's treatment, and in this poem he discarded Malory's story for the earlier versions he had learned to know in his wide reading—the French versions and the mediaeval English rhymed romance of *Sir Tristrem*, edited and completed by Sir Walter Scott in 1804, which followed the story of Thomas of Britain. Swinburne kept the story that Iseult

of Brittany deceived Tristram about the color of the sails, so that he died before his beloved reached him, and he emphasized the neglected wife's not unreasonable hate. His characters have none of the patience and control of Arnold's. The scene of the love potion shows them completely abandoned to their emotion:

> Their heads neared, and their hands were drawn in one,
> And they saw dark, though still the unsunken sun
> Far through fine rain shot fire into the south;
> And their four lips became one burning mouth.

The imagery is repeated in a death scene which moves almost as swiftly at the end as in the old romance. Iseult, reaching Tristram too late,

> came and stood above him newly dead,
> And felt his death upon her: and her head
> Bowed, as to reach the spring that slakes all drouth;
> And their four lips became one silent mouth.

Wagner wrote the libretto of his opera *Tristan and Isolde* in 1857, the year when Morris began work on his Oxford painting and Swinburne published the single canto of his youthful *Queen Yseult*. The music was composed in 1859 and the opera was first produced in 1865. *Tristan and Isolde* was the first adequate expression in music of a great Arthurian story. Arthurian masques and plays had often been accompanied by incidental music, and Arthurian ballets had been given in France. In England Dryden's *King Arthur, the British Worthy*, produced in 1691, had had music by Purcell, but the music had no essential relation to the action. In Wagner's operas, however, music and drama were blended to convey the emotions of the characters.

Wagner's *Tristan* was based on Gottfried von Strassburg's early thirteenth-century romance of Tristan. There were, naturally, many omissions and changes for dramatic emphasis. The first and last acts were determined by the outstanding scenes of the romances—the drinking of the love potion and the lovers' death. For the second act the composer combined the many love scenes into one.

The opera begins on shipboard while Tristan is taking Isolde to Cornwall. She is restless and unhappy and blames Tristan for the death of her kinsman Morolt and her own banishment to a foreign land. Actually, she already loves him but will not admit it. To distract her attention Brangaene shows her a casket containing the love potion and other draughts prepared by the Queen of Ireland, among them a flask of poison. Isolde sees a way out of her unhappiness. She bids Brangaene prepare a poisoned drink and summons Tristan to share it. He understands her intent and, already loving her, accepts the cup. Before he has finished, Isolde snatches it from his hand and drains it—but Brangaene has substituted the love potion. Wagner uses the potion merely as a means of making the lovers realize their love. As they await death together, they find that love, not death, has overtaken them.

Wagner's stage directions were very explicit. For this act they call for a scene very similar to that of Rossetti's picture—"a pavilion erected on the deck of a ship." During the drinking of the potion the pavilion is cut off by curtains from the rest of the ship, to suggest that the lovers are shut into a world of their own emotion. At other times the curtains are lifted or drawn apart, revealing "the whole length of the ship . . . down to the stern, with the sea and horizon beyond it," as in Rossetti's picture.

The circumstances attending the great love scene in the second act resemble most closely those of the tryst at the fountain so popular in the Middle Ages. To condense the action and heighten the dramatic effect, Wagner combined the moonlight tryst with Gottfried's scene of discovery and farewell, which takes place much later in the romance. At the suggestion of the jealous Melot, Mark has pretended to go hunting, to give the lovers an opportunity to meet. The meeting place is the garden of the castle at Tintagel, but there is no fountain, and instead of hiding in a tree, Mark enters the garden with dignity. Here again Wagner gave detailed directions, in which light and darkness play important parts. The light which Isolde extinguishes as a signal for Tristan to come is no mere torch but a symbol of the day which parts them. The darkness that follows represents the

A setting for the second act of Wagner's "Tristan and Isolde," showing Isolde and Brangaene on the stage. Designed by Adolphe Appia in 1895; adapted for the production of the opera given at Milan in 1923

night which brings them together and their final union in death. In his setting for this act, Adolphe Appia used light and shadow rather than painted scenery. Brangaene, in this sketch, is going toward the stairway to take up her watch before Isolde summons Tristan. She has already warned her mistress that she thinks there is danger. But Isolde extinguishes the torch and Tristan enters the garden. The music of the scene which follows ebbs and flows in a tide of passion. The lovers' duet reaches a climax of emotion in words which come close to Iseult's farewell in Gottfried's romance: "Tristan and Iseult, thou and I, we twain are but one being, without distinction or difference." Mark and his men enter the garden, the lovers' passionate duet is cut short, and Tristan falls wounded by Melot, who betrayed him.

In the last act Tristan dies in his castle across the sea. To concentrate attention upon the hero and heroine, Wagner omitted all mention of Iseult of Brittany and the story of the black and white sails. Isolde reaches her lover in time for a farewell and dies upon his body, singing the praise of the death which finally unites them.

The Lady of the Lake stealing the infant Lancelot. Manuscript illumination, XV century, from a French prose romance of Lancelot. In the Bibliothèque Nationale, Paris, Fr. 13, fol. 156

LANCELOT AND GUENEVERE

Lancelot, chief knight of the Round Table, was a creation of mediaeval romancers, who found material for their tales in Celtic mythology. The oldest existing romance of Lancelot is Chrétien de Troyes's *Knight of the Cart*, composed about 1170, but as this tells only one part of the hero's long history some complete story must have been known before. The early thirteenth-century French prose romance of Lancelot was the source for most of the later versions. It begins with Lancelot's early life, but its central motive is his love for Guenevere.

The opening chapters of the prose romance tell of Lancelot's childhood, which Malory neglects entirely. The child's mother, weeping over the body of her husband, King Ban, left her little son by the shore of a lake that "had been named from the days of the pagans the Lake of Diana." Returning, she saw a damsel playing with the child, who "was the fairest babe in all the world." As the queen drew near, the damsel "rose with the child in her arms, and she went speedily down to the lake, and she put her feet together, and she sprang thereinto."

"Now the story saith that the damsel that carried Lancelot into the lake was a fay. In those days all maidens that knew enchantments or charms were called fays, and there were many of them at this time, and more in Great Britain than in other lands." So powerful a fay was this damsel that the lake itself "was naught but enchantment. . . . In the part where the lake seemed widest and deepest the Lady had many fair and noble dwellings. . . . And her abode was so hidden that none might find it, for the semblance of the lake covered it." There Lancelot dwelt with the Lady of the Lake and her maidens until he was eighteen, and from this dwelling he got the name Lancelot of the Lake. The Lady had the boy taught all the arts of courtly life, but she could not make him a knight, and she knew that "if she kept him from knighthood after the proper age, she would commit a mortal sin." So she took him to Arthur's court at Camelot, and there "both the king and the queen came to meet him, and they took him each by the hand." Lancelot "marvelled greatly whence so great beauty might come as he saw in her," and "when he felt her touch him, he trembled even as if he awoke from sleep. . . . And then the queen perceived that he was abashed and full of thought, but she ne'er believed that it was for her sake, and none the less she suspected it somewhat, and she left him be." Arthur knighted the young squire, but forgot to gird on the knightly sword. Thereupon Lancelot rode away upon his first adventure, but the queen sent after him "a right good sword with a richly wrought scabbard and girdle" and Lancelot declared "that now, thanks to God and his lady, he was a knight." So the romancer made the hero Guenevere's special knight.

The knighting of Lancelot is a perfect introduction to the theme of love as twelfth-century court poets portrayed it. Their idea of love was natural in a time when the marriages of high-born ladies were arranged with little or no regard for love. To counterbalance this lack there grew up the code known as courtly love, in which a knight vowed his lifelong devotion to a noble lady, usually married and often older than he, and sought glory and renown for her sake. Judging from the courtly writings of the time, no fair and noble lady could be without such a knight. In the chronicles the traitor Mordred had been Guenevere's lover, but such a villain was unworthy in the eyes of the romancers, and Lancelot was created to fill the role. In describing the lovers' emotions twelfth-century court poets were influenced by the sophisticated, pagan love poems of Ovid, one of the Latin authors most widely read in the Middle Ages. But there were conflicts in the mediaeval world unknown to Ovid's day—conflicts between the great loyalties of chivalry, to God, to overlord, and to lady. Even the ideal courtly love story of Lancelot and Guenevere could not remain untouched by such contradictory ties. Lancelot's love was a violation of his obligations to Arthur as his king, and helped to destroy the fellowship of the Round Table; it was a violation of God's law, and cost him his chance of achieving the Grail, the symbol of spiritual satisfaction—for of the three loyalties he could be wholly true to only one, love for his lady.

In the happy springtime of this love Lancelot left Camelot to seek renown for Guenevere's sake. Soon he

captured singlehanded a castle known as Dolorous Gard because of the many knights killed or imprisoned there. Within the castle he found three silver shields marked with red bends, which he took as his own heraldic device. He made this castle his dwelling and changed its name to Joyous Gard, but he would not return to Arthur's court until he had distinguished himself by still more marvelous deeds.

After many adventures he entered, unknown, into a joust between Arthur's knights and the men of Prince Galehot, who had challenged the king. In this joust Lancelot won both great renown and the friendship of Galehot, who, for his sake, made peace with Arthur. Guenevere was curious about the distinguished, unknown knight, so Galehot brought Lancelot to her one evening as she sat in a meadow with two ladies. There the queen questioned him so closely concerning the lady for whom he did such daring deeds that he replied at last: "I see that I must needs say it. It was ye." With that he grew so pale that Galehot came running from a little distance, where he had sat talking with the ladies and his seneschal, and besought the queen to take Lancelot as her knight, saying, "Do ye kiss him in my sight for the beginning of true love."

"As for kissing, said she, I see not that this is either the place or the time. And doubt not that I would be as fain for it as he would be, but yonder are those ladies, who marvel much that we are gone so far, and it could not be that they would not see it. And yet, if it is his pleasure, I will kiss him gladly.

"And the knight was so glad that he could answer naught save, Lady, gramercy.

"Ah, lady, said Galehot, doubt not his will thereto, for it is wholly there. And wit ye well that none will see it. Now let us three draw together even as if we were taking counsel together.

"Now wherefore should I wait for entreaties? said the queen. More do I desire it than either ye or he.

"Therewithal they all three drew together and made semblance that they took counsel. The queen saw that

The first kiss of Lancelot and Guenevere. Manuscript illumination, about 1310, from a French prose romance of Lancelot. In the Pierpont Morgan Library, New York, MS 805, fol. 67

the knight durst do no more, and she raised his chin, and she kissed him full long in the presence of Galehot."

The miniature above shows this first kiss. The slender, graceful figures of Lancelot and the queen, leaning toward each other with outstretched arms across Galehot's knees, are silhouetted against a background of bright gold; in the meadow at the right conventionalized trees on a ground of diamond-patterned rose make an idyllic setting for the dainty ladies and the youthful seneschal.

"Thus the first meeting of Lancelot and the queen was by means of Galehot. . . . Then they arose all three, and already it drew fast toward night, but the moon was arisen, and it was so light that they might see clearly the length of the meadow."

Soon after, Lancelot took his place in the household of Arthur, and when the king had conquered Gaul he invested the knight with the French lands. But Lancelot remained Guenevere's own knight, ready to carry out her slightest wish—and he had many opportunities to serve her. Of all his deeds, the most famous were his rescues of the queen. Several times a king or a prince stole her away and always, for one reason or another, it was Lancelot rather than Arthur who rescued her.

One of these stories of rescue was the subject of Chrétien de Troyes's *Lancelot*, or *The Knight of the Cart*, so-called because, in order to reach Guenevere's prison, the hero rode in a cart. This, according to the author, was shameful, since carts were used as pillories for the punishment of petty criminals, but Lancelot regarded it only as a trial of true love. In the manuscript illumination at the top of page 54 the hero bears a shield that is not his own. Sir Gawain is riding behind the cart, one squire carrying his shield and another his helmet.

At the end of the journey Lancelot came to a river

53

ABOVE: *Lancelot rides in a cart to reach the castle where Guenevere is imprisoned.* BELOW: *Lancelot crosses the Sword Bridge to rescue the queen. Manuscript illuminations, about 1310, from a French prose romance of Lancelot. In the Pierpont Morgan Library, New York, MS 805, fols. 158, 166*

across which lay the castle where the queen was held. Chrétien's description of the stream is vivid. The river, he says, "is as swift and raging, as black and turgid, as fierce and terrible as if it were the devil's stream; and it is so dangerous and bottomless that anything falling into it would be as completely lost as if it fell into the salt sea. And the bridge, which spans it, is different from any other bridge. . . . The bridge across the cold stream consisted of a polished, gleaming sword." Two lions seemed to guard the further end. Lancelot removed the armor from his hands and feet to get a firmer grasp of the blade, and thus "he passes over with great pain and agony, being wounded in the hands, knees, and feet. But even this suffering is sweet to him: for Love, who conducts and leads him on, assuages and relieves the pain. Creeping on his hands, feet, and knees, he proceeds until he reaches the other side." Then he remembered the lions, but they were nowhere to be seen.

The miniature below is from a prose romance that differs in some details from Chrétien's poem. In the prose version Lancelot's companions "laced the sides of his hauberk together and sewed them with great threads of iron that they had brought, and his gauntlets likewise they sewed within on his hands, and his boots beneath. . . . And he went straight to the bridge and he looked toward the tower where the queen was captive, and he bowed his head before it, and thereafter he crossed him, and he put his shield behind his back that it might not hinder him." Then as he came near the shore "he looked and he saw a villein that led two lions by one chain, and they made such a noise that they might be heard afar"—but these beasts were only enchantments.

o Lancelot came to the castle of King Baudemagus, whose son, Meleagant, had stolen Guenevere, and there he defeated that prince. In the miniature Lancelot bears his red-banded shield slung across his back, as described in the prose romance. Blood drips from his feet and hands, which are covered with mail. A peasant holds the two curly-maned, imaginary lions on a chain, Guenevere and King Baudemagus look on from the tower, and at the right they welcome Lancelot.

This scene became a symbol among mediaeval artists of the power and constancy of love, and was a favorite in many forms of art. It was carved on a capital of the fourteenth-century church of St. Peter at Caen, where a single lion guards the bridge and only Guenevere's head appears above the battlements of the tower. The scene is also carved on several fourteenth-century ivory caskets, combined with adventures of Gawain. Gawain came to a castle in which many maidens were held captive and was led to a chamber where was a bed set on wheels and hung round with bells. He lay down upon it

ABOVE: *Lancelot crosses the Sword Bridge. Carved capital, French, XIV century. In the church of St. Peter, Caen.* BELOW: *Lancelot crosses the Sword Bridge; adventures of Gawain. Ivory casket, French, XIV century. In the Metropolitan Museum*

fully armed, and soon the bells rang, bolts and arrows shot into the room, and a lion sprang at him. He killed the lion, cutting off one paw, which remained stuck in his shield. The damsels, then set free from captivity, trooped to thank him. In the casket illustrated below, the scene at the left shows Gawain fighting the lion; then comes Lancelot crossing the Sword Bridge, his feet covered with mail, his hands bare; next is Gawain upon the magic bed, with a rain of darts falling about him; and finally the grateful maidens. Darts are also falling upon Lancelot on the Sword Bridge; they were probably introduced merely to make the central panels balance.

Lancelot's fame as a warrior was so great that in tour-

Lancelot fights a tournament in disguise. Manuscript illumination, about 1310, from a French prose romance of Lancelot. In the Pierpont Morgan Library, New York, MS 805, fol. 239

naments and jousts his opponents were often terrified by his very name, so that he sometimes fought in disguise, bearing a shield without the heraldic blazons by which knights could be identified in combat when the visors of their helmets were closed. The miniature above shows him carrying a plain white shield at a tournament to prove that it was his strength and skill and not his reputation which had made him the most renowned knight of the Round Table. He appears four times, riding from left to right, and at the end fighting with another knight who also bears a blank shield.

So brave and courteous a knight was naturally loved by many ladies, but his heart remained Guenevere's alone. Elaine of Carbonek won him for a little while by a stratagem which made him believe her to be Guenevere. The fair maid of Astolat, who was nameless in the early stories, but whom Malory calls Elaine, loved him too, and died because he could not love her.

As Malory tells the tale of Elaine, Lancelot set out alone for a tournament in which he wished no one, not even his own kin, to know that he was fighting. On his way he came to Astolat, where he lodged with an old baron, Sir Bernard of Astolat, who did not recognize him. Lancelot asked Sir Bernard if he might borrow a shield "not openly known." The old baron lent him the shield of his eldest son, Sir Tirre, who had been hurt in his first tournament, so that his shield was known nowhere but at home, and Sir Lavaine, the baron's younger son, rode with Lancelot to the tournament.

"This old baron had a daughter that was called that time the fair maiden of Astolat. And ever she beheld Sir Launcelot wonderfully; and as the book saith, she cast such a love unto Sir Launcelot that she could never

withdraw her love, wherefore she died, and her name was Elaine le Blank," which means the white or fair. The young Elaine le Blank "besought Sir Launcelot to wear upon him at the jousts a token of hers." Now Lancelot, from loyalty to Guenevere, had never worn a lady's token at a tournament and at first he refused. "Then he remembered him he would go to the jousts disguised. And by cause he had never fore that time borne no manner of token of no damosel, then he bethought him that he would bear one of her, that none of his blood thereby might know him, and then he said: Fair maiden, I will grant you to wear a token of yours upon mine helmet, and therefore what it is, shew it me. Sir, she said, it is a red sleeve of mine of scarlet, well embroidered with great pearls: and so she brought it him. So Sir Launcelot received it, and said: Never did I erst so much for no damosel. And then Sir Launcelot betook the fair maiden his shield in keeping, and prayed her to keep that until that he came again." But she did not know why he had never before worn a maiden's token nor why he wore hers now.

Lancelot and Sir Lavaine rode to the tournament, and there Lancelot bore down all who attacked him, so that many wondered who this strange knight could be and would have believed him to be Lancelot except for the sleeve upon his helmet. Finally his own kinsmen, angry that a stranger should equal or even surpass the deeds of Lancelot, set upon him, and one of them, Sir Bors, wounded him sorely. Yet Lancelot overthrew them all and was awarded the prize. But he was so deeply wounded that, instead of waiting to receive it, he rode with Lavaine to a hermitage to be healed.

Meanwhile Gawain, encouraged by Arthur, set out to find the strange knight. By chance he too came to Astolat, where he told of the prowess of the knight with the red sleeve. "Now blessed be God, said the fair maiden of Astolat, that that knight sped so well, for he is the man in the world that I first loved, and truly he shall be last that ever I shall love. . . . And here with me

left his own shield." Straightway Sir Gawain asked
for a sight of this shield, and he knew it at once for
Lancelot's. So he returned to tell the court that Lancelot had been the victor in the tournament and that he
had worn the sleeve of the fair maid of Astolat. When
Guenevere heard "that it were marvel to tell the great
love that is between the fair maiden of Astolat and him,"
she "was nigh out of her mind for wrath," for she was
sure that Lancelot loved her no more. But Sir Bors,
grieving, set out to find Lancelot.

Meanwhile Elaine had heard that her knight lay
somewhere sorely hurt and had won her father's permission to search for him. By chance she came upon her
brother Lavaine, who led her to the hermitage. When
she saw Lancelot "so sick and pale in his bed she might
not speak, but suddenly she fell to the earth. . . . And
then Sir Launcelot prayed Sir Lavaine to take her up:
and bring her to me. And when she came to herself
Sir Launcelot kissed her, and said: Fair maiden, why fare
ye thus? ye put me to pain; wherefore make ye no more
such cheer, for an ye be come to comfort me ye be right
welcome." And so Elaine and her brother stayed with
Lancelot, and she "watched him day and night, and did
such attendance to him, that the French book saith there
was never woman did more kindlier for man than she."

There Sir Bors found her when he came at last to the
hermitage where Lancelot lay, and he said, "Is this she
. . . that men call the fair maiden of Astolat? She it is,
said Launcelot, that by no means I cannot put her
from me. Why should ye put her from you? said Sir
Bors, she is a passing fair damosel, and a well bisene,
and well taught; and God would, fair cousin, said Sir
Bors, that ye could love her, but as to that I may not,
nor dare not, counsel you. But I see well, said Sir Bors,
by her diligence about you that she loveth you entirely.
That me repenteth, said Sir Launcelot."

When Lancelot was well, he returned to Astolat.
And so upon the morn when Sir Launcelot should
depart, fair Elaine brought her father with her, and
Sir Lavaine, and Sir Tirre, and thus she said:

"My lord, Sir Launcelot, now I see ye will depart;
now fair knight and courteous knight, have mercy upon
me, and suffer me not to die for thy love. What would
ye that I did? said Sir Launcelot. I would have you to
my husband, said Elaine. Fair damosel, I thank you, said
Sir Launcelot, but truly, said he, I cast me never to be
wedded man. Then, fair knight, said she, will ye be my
paramour? Jesu defend me, said Sir Launcelot, for then
I rewarded your father and your brother full evil for
their great goodness. Alas, said she, then must I die for
your love. . . . Then she shrieked shrilly, and fell down
in a swoon; and then women bare her into her chamber."
And Lancelot returned to Arthur's court and Sir
Lavaine went with him.

But the maid of Astolat sorrowed day and night and
slept not at all nor ate nor drank. When ten days had

*The body of the maid of Astolat comes to Arthur's
court. Manuscript illumination, about 1316, from a
French prose romance. In the British Museum, Add. MS
10294, fol. 65*

passed, a priest gave her the rites for the dying—but
still she spoke of Lancelot. "Then her ghostly father bad
her leave such thoughts. Then she said, why should I
leave such thoughts? Am I not an earthly woman?"
And she called her father and her brother, and asked
them to write in a letter what she would tell them, and
when she was dead to close her hand upon it, robe her
in her richest garments, and place her in a fair bed in a
barge covered with black samite, with one trusted man
to steer it to Arthur's court. (According to the version
in the thirteenth-century Italian *novellino* "How the
Lady of Scalot died for love of Lancelot of the Lake,"
the boat had "no oars, sails, or steersman.")

When Elaine was dead, her father and brother did as
she had desired. King Arthur and Queen Guenevere,
looking out of the palace window, saw the black barge
and went down to look at it. They saw, says Malory,
"the fairest woman lie in a rich bed, covered unto her
middle with many rich clothes, and all was of cloth of
gold, and she lay as though she had smiled." The queen
saw the letter in the maiden's hand and Arthur "made
a clerk to read it, and this was the intent of the letter.
Most noble knight, Sir Launcelot, now hath death made
us two at debate for your love. I was your lover, that
men called the fair maiden of Astolat; therefore unto
all ladies I make my moan, yet pray for my soul and bury
me at least, and offer ye my mass-penny: this is my last
request. And a clene maiden I died, I take God to wit-
ness: pray for my soul, Sir Launcelot, as thou art peer-
less. . . . The king, the queen, and all the knights wept
for pity," and "upon the morn she was interred richly,
and Sir Launcelot offered her mass-penny; and all the

knights of the Table Round that were there at that time offered with Sir Launcelot. . . . Then the queen sent for Sir Launcelot, and prayed him of mercy, for why that she had been wroth with him causeless. This is not the first time, said Sir Launcelot, that ye had been displeased with me causeless."

So Lancelot and Guenevere were reconciled, but their love was more troubled than before. Not only had the queen's jealousy of Elaine come between them, but her power over Lancelot had caused his failure in the quest of the Holy Grail, and he could not forget his vision of the spiritual joy he could not win.

Jealousy and suspicion had grown among the knights of the Round Table, too. Finally Mordred and his half-brother, Agravaine, who had long brewed mischief, denounced the lovers to Arthur and attacked Lancelot in Guenevere's chamber. The knight, though unarmed, fought his way to safety, but Guenevere remained in her enemies' hands. Arthur's grief, as Malory describes it, seems more for Lancelot than for the queen: "Alas, me sore repenteth, said the king, that ever Sir Launcelot should be against me. Now I am sure the noble fellowship of the Round Table is broken for ever, for with him will many a noble knight hold." Arthur condemned Guenevere to death at the stake, but Lancelot and his friends rescued her and carried her to Joyous Gard. Arthur besieged him there, though unwillingly, for he thought often "on the great courtesy that was in Sir Launcelot more than in any other man." And Launcelot lamented: "I have no heart to fight against my lord Arthur, for ever meseemeth I do not as I ought to do." Finally the Pope commanded Arthur to take Guenevere back with honor, and Lancelot departed across the sea to France. As Arthur had foretold, many good knights went with Lancelot, although he besought them to stay with the king, telling them that Mordred meant treachery.

Arthur gathered an army and followed Lancelot to France, spurred on by Gawain because Lancelot had killed his brothers while rescuing Guenevere. This was Mordred's opportunity. He seized the kingdom and declared that he would marry Guenevere. The queen shut herself in the Tower of London. Arthur came quickly back to London, but with only a remnant of his knights, for many had fallen fighting Lancelot. The king won his last battle, but he saw Guenevere no more.

Guenevere, when she heard that Arthur was dead, entered a nunnery. Lancelot hastened back to England to help Arthur, only to hear of the king's death. In the early prose romance he was also told that Guenevere was dead, and he retired straightway to a hermitage. But a last, poignant farewell scene had crept into the story long before Malory wrote. As he tells it, Lancelot set out in search of Guenevere, and "at the last he came to a nunnery, and then was Queen Guenever ware of Sir Launcelot as he walked in the cloister. And when she saw

him there she swooned thrice, that all the ladies and gentlewomen had work enough to hold the queen up. . . When Sir Launcelot was brought to her, then she said to all the ladies: Through this man and me hath all this war been wrought, and the death of the most noblest knights of the world; for through our love that we have loved together is my most noble lord slain. . . . Therefore, Sir Launcelot, I require of thee and beseech thee heartily, for all the love that ever was betwixt us, that thou never see me more . . . for as well as I have loved thee, mine heart will not serve me to see thee, for through thee and me is the flower of kings and knights destroyed; therefore, Sir Launcelot, go to thy realm, and there take thee a wife, and live with her with joy and bliss. . . Now, sweet madam, said Sir Launcelot, would ye that I should now return again unto my country, and there to wed a lady? Nay, madam, wit you well that shall I never do, . . . but the same destiny that ye have taken you to, I will take me unto. . . . And therefore, lady, sithen ye have taken you to perfection, I must needs take me to perfection, of right. For I take record of God, in you have I had mine earthly joy; and if I had found you now so disposed, I had cast to have had you into mine own realm. . . . Wherefore, madam, I pray you kiss me and never no more. Nay, said the queen, that shall I never do, but abstain you from such works: and they departed."

Lancelot went his way, weeping, and came to a hermitage, where he dwelt with Bedivere and Bors and seven other knights of the Round Table. At the end of seven years there came to him a vision that Guenevere was dead and that he should take her and bury her beside Arthur. So he went with his fellows to the nunnery and carried the queen to Glastonbury and laid her beside the king. After this Lancelot "ate but little meat, ne drank, till he was dead." Six weeks after Guenevere's death the hermit dreamed that he "saw the angels heave up Sir Launcelot unto heaven," and when he went to Lancelot's cell he "found him stark dead, and he lay as he had smiled." So Lancelot's companions took him and buried him as he had desired at Joyous Gard, and there Sir Ector de Maris bade him farewell in words which might have served as a lament for mediaeval chivalry:

"Ah Launcelot, he said, thou were head of all Christian knights, and now I dare say, said Sir Ector, thou Sir Launcelot, there thou liest, that thou were never matched of earthly knight's hand. And thou were the courteoust knight that ever bare shield. And thou were the truest friend to thy lover that ever bestrad horse. And thou were the truest lover of a sinful man that ever loved woman. And thou were the kindest man that ever struck with sword. And thou were the goodliest person that ever came among press of knights. And thou was the meekest man and the gentlest that ever ate in hall among ladies. And thou were the sternest knight to thy mortal foe that ever put spear in the rest."

efer sepelire la regina agrando honore et esso se desarmo de tute sue arme, lesole apci scrain
par le grand diserto de Dinatee et esendo alla badia de speciale la dove erane emonsti et
eraque emonace boso lo casto/carmo quello abitre equi steti Lanyloto aserature adio estete

mendeo ta per mes, et apsse morte, succedoto, came le nro libre pone fine atute le st
avie le quale ferano fitte y la dict erane Jupere che apertamente Luio dimostrato et
.... questo libro fato p Saliano di Anzoli fo buta m/ aij. cccc. xlvj. adi xv de luio

*The farewell of Lancelot and Guenevere; Lancelot en-
ters a hermitage. Pen drawings, North Italian, 1446,
from an Italian prose romance of the Round Table. In
the Biblioteca Nazionale, Florence, Cod. Pal. 556*

Guenevere. Study of Jane Burden by Dante Gabriel Rossetti, 1858, for his painting in the Oxford Union. National Gallery of Ireland, Dublin

Guenevere fascinated poets of the nineteenth century as she had the romancers of the Middle Ages, but their interest was in fresh interpretations of character rather than in action. Much had changed since the twelfth century, when the courtly poets had treated love and marriage as two separate relationships; by the nineteenth, they were regarded as the same, since marriage for love rather than for convenience had become the recognized English ideal. Between the Middle Ages and Tennyson's time lay, also, the Reformation, the stern religious teachings of Calvin, and the eighteenth-century Wesleyan revival. All these had put emphasis upon an individual sense of sin and had condemned most vigorously unfaithfulness in marriage. As a result of all these changes, where the mediaeval Guenevere had felt remorse chiefly because of the disaster she had brought about, in the nineteenth century she was tormented by a sense of personal guilt as well. There is less difference in Lancelot, whose character had been more fully developed in the romances.

Tennyson's first treatment of the story of the queen and her knight was in the short poem *Sir Launcelot and Queen Guinevere* in 1842. Here Guenevere rides with

Lancelot in "the boyhood of the year." There is no word of love between them, but it is implied in the magic of the springtime and in the lines:

> A man had given all other bliss,
> And all his worldly worth for this,
> To waste his whole heart on one kiss
> Upon her perfect lips.

But when he told the end of the story in *Guinevere*, in 1859, he made Arthur the symbol of the best in the human soul, passing over all the blemishes which Malory had shown, including the king's own unfaithfulness to his wife and his sentence that she be burnt at the stake.

Yet Tennyson could not make Guenevere an evil figure, so he devised new excuses for her. He said that Arthur sent Lancelot to bring her to Camelot and that she thought at first that he was Arthur and learned to love him before her marriage to the king.

There is no farewell between Lancelot and Guenevere in *The Idylls of the King:* Tennyson invented, instead, a farewell between Arthur and Guenevere in the convent to which the queen had fled after Mordred's denunciation. Guenevere, repentant, grovels at the king's feet, and when Arthur has finally gone, she cries:

> "now I see thee what thou art,
> Thou art the highest and most human too,
> Not Lancelot, nor another. Is there none
> Will tell the King I love him, tho' so late?"

It was in keeping with the conventions of the poet's time that the queen should discover she loved her husband rather than Lancelot.

William Morris's poem *King Arthur's Tomb*, published the year before Tennyson's *Guinevere*, followed Malory in showing Guenevere's repentance through her farewell to Lancelot. The scene is changed, however, from a convent to Arthur's tomb at Glastonbury. The poem was inspired by Rossetti's picture, opposite, painted in 1854. After a descriptive opening, it moves swiftly, in snatches of dramatic dialogue, broken by Guenevere's anguished murmurs to herself, which reveal her love for the man whom she is tormenting. Suddenly overcome by horror at her sin, she has determined to save her lover's soul and her own by rousing him to a remorse which will separate them forever. Lancelot arrived at Glastonbury to meet Guenevere.

> Dazed there he laid his head upon a tomb
> Not knowing it was Arthur's, at which sight
> One of her maidens told her, "He is come,"
> And she went forth to meet him, yet a blight
>
> Had settled on her, all her robes were black,
> With a long white veil only; she went slow,
> As one walks to be slain . . . .
> . . . .
> He did not hear her coming, as he lay
> On Arthur's head, till some of her long hair
> Brush'd on the new-cut stone—"Well done! to pray
>
> "For Arthur, my dear lord, the greatest king
> That ever lived." "Guenevere! Guenevere!

Do you not know me, are you gone mad? fling
Your arms and hair about me, lest I fear

"You are not Guenevere, but some other thing."
"Pray you forgive me, fair lord Launcelot!
I am not mad, but I am sick; they cling,
God's curses, unto such as I am; not

"Ever again shall we twine arms and lips."
"Yea, she is mad: thy heavy law, O Lord,
Is very tight about her now, and grips
Her poor heart, so that no right word

"Can reach her mouth; so, Lord, forgive her now,
That she, not knowing what she does, being mad,
Kills me in this way—Guenevere, bend low
And kiss me once! for God's love kiss me! sad

"Though your face is, you look much kinder now;
Yea once, once for the last time, kiss me, lest I die!"
"Christ! my hot lips are very near his brow,
Help me to save his soul!—Yea, verily,

"Across my husband's head, fair Launcelot!
Fair serpent mark'd with V upon the head!
This thing we did while yet he was alive,
Why not, O twisting knight, now he is dead?

. . . .

"Launcelot, Launcelot, why did he take your hand,
When he had kissed me in his kingly way?
Saying, 'This is the knight whom all the land
Calls Arthur's banner, sword, and shield to-day.'

. . . .

"I shall go mad,
Or else die kissing him, he is so pale;
He thinks me mad already, O bad! bad!
Let me lie down a little while and wail!"

"No longer so, rise up, I pray you, love,
And slay me really, then we shall be heal'd,
Perchance, in the aftertime by God above."
"Banner of Arthur—with black-bended shield

"Sinister-wise across a fair gold ground!
Here let me tell you what a knight you are,
O sword and shield of Arthur! you are found
A crooked sword, I think, that leaves a scar.

. . . .

"Banner, and sword, and shield, you dare not pray to die,
Lest you meet Arthur in the other world,
And, knowing who you are, he pass you by
Taking short turns that he may watch you curl'd,

"Body and face and limbs in agony,
Lest he weep presently and go away,
Saying, 'I loved him once,' with a sad sigh—
Now I have slain him, Lord, let me go too, I pray.
                              [Launcelot falls.]
"Alas! alas! I know not what to do,
If I run fast it is perchance that I
May fall and stun myself, much better so,
Never, never again! not even when I die."

61

Lancelot and the Lady of Shalott. Illustration by Dante Gabriel Rossetti for an edition of Tennyson's poems published by Edward Moxon, London, 1857. Slightly enlarged

After the sharp passion of Lancelot and Guenevere the love of the maid of Astolat is like quiet in the midst of storm. The old story of the nameless maid was the source for Tennyson's early lyric *The Lady of Shalott*, published in 1832. It furnished, however, merely a framework for the poet's inventions and allegories. Years afterward Tennyson wrote in the notes he prepared for his poems: "*The Lady of Shalott*. From an Italian novelette, *Donna di Scalotta*. Shalott and Astolat are the same words. . . . Shalott was a softer sound than 'Scalott.'" This novelette was some form of the *novellino* "How the Lady of Scalot died for love of Lancelot of the Lake," from the late thirteenth-century Italian compilation known as the *Cento Novelle Antiche*, or "Hundred Old Tales." Tennyson may have read it in the original or in a translation by Thomas Roscoe, published in 1825, or in both.

Tennyson's Lady of Shalott, living alone upon an island in the river,

> has heard a whisper say,
> A curse is on her if she stay
> To look down to Camelot.

So she wove steadily upon a magic web, seeing the world only as shadows passing through her mirror until she glimpsed Sir Lancelot riding to Camelot. She looked after him and then:

> Out flew the web and floated wide;
> The mirror crack'd from side to side;
> "The curse is come upon me," cried
> The Lady of Shalott.

Tennyson's own interpretation was that the sight of the real world took the Lady "out of the region of shadow into that of realities." But in the world of realities she could not live, so she laid her down in a boat and died singing, as the stream bore her to Camelot. There

> Out upon the wharfs they came,
> Knight and burgher, lord and dame,
> And round the prow they read her name,
> *The Lady of Shalott.*
> . . . .
> But Lancelot mused a little space;
> He said, "She has a lovely face;
> God in his mercy lend her grace,
> The Lady of Shalott."

The curse, the web, the song, and the idea that the Lady had seen Lancelot only at a distance were Tennyson's contributions; the mirror may have been suggested by the magic mirror made by Merlin in Spenser's *Faerie Queene*.

Like the poem, Rossetti's illustration suggests solitude and remoteness. Lancelot and the Lady are far removed from the world about them. The figures on the wharf in the background are very small, as though at a great distance, and those close by are suggested by details of hands, feet, or faces. The two chief characters, brought together for the first and last time at Camelot, seem isolated in a world of their own, far from the suggested throngs.

Tennyson told the story of Malory's maid of Astolat in his idyll of *Elaine* in 1859. Tennyson's Elaine is less direct and robust than Malory's, more given to dreams. She knew that Lancelot wore her token not from love but as a disguise, yet she treasured his shield in her tower and "so lived in fantasy," embroidering for it a silken case and imagining the deeds which had produced its scars. Her doubts and final desperate declaration of love to Lancelot measure the difference between the mediaeval maid's direct approach to a situation not uncommon in her time and the anguish of a Victorian girl driven by strong emotion to break the conventions which forbade a woman to take the initiative in love. Tennyson's Elaine came to Lancelot alone, not with her father and brother, as in Malory:

> Then suddenly and passionately she spoke:
> "I have gone mad. I love you; let me die."
> "Ah, sister," answer'd Lancelot, "what is this?"
> And innocently extending her white arms,
> "Your love," she said, "your love—to be your wife."

Lancelot refused gently both this offer and her final plea:

"I care not to be wife,
But to be with you still, to see your face,
To serve you, and to follow you thro'
    the world."

Then he added a note entirely foreign to mediaeval romance: "This is not love, but love's first flash in youth." And to discourage what he believed to be a youthful infatuation, he rode away with no gesture of farewell although he knew that she was watching him.

Elaine sat alone in her tower. Lancelot's
            very shield was gone; only the case,
Her own poor work, her empty labor, left.
But still she heard him, still his picture
    form'd
And grew between her and the pictured
    wall.

In her deep hurt she sickened to her death, and at the last besought Lavaine to write her letter to Lancelot and put it in her hand. And then she said:

    "Let there be prepared a chariot-bier
To take me to the river, and a barge
Be ready on the river, clothed in black.
I go in state to court to meet the Queen.
There surely I shall speak for mine own
    self,
And none of you can speak for me so well.
And therefore let our dumb old man alone
Go with me; he can steer and row, and he
Will guide me to that palace, to the doors."

After her death Elaine's brothers carried her to the barge
    And on the black decks laid her in her bed,
    Set in her hand a lily, o'er her hung
    The silken case with braided blazonings.
    . . . .
    Then rose the dumb old servitor, and the dead,
    Oar'd by the dumb, went upward with the flood—
    In her right hand the lily, in her left
    The letter—all her bright hair streaming down—
    And all the coverlid was cloth of gold
    Drawn to her waist, and she herself in white
    All but her face, and that clear-featured face
    Was lovely, for she did not seem as dead,
    But fast asleep, and lay as tho' she smiled.

The old man rowed the barge to Camelot, where Perceval and Galahad carried the maid to Arthur's hall.
    Then came the fine Gawain and wonder'd at her,
    And Lancelot later came and mused at her,
    But Arthur saw the letter in her hand.

Elaine's letter reads:
    "Most noble lord, Sir Lancelot of the Lake,
    I, sometime call'd the maid of Astolat,
    Come, for you left me taking no farewell,
    Hither, to take my last farewell of you.
    I loved you, and my love had no return,
    And therefore my true love has been my death.
    And therefore to our Lady Guinevere,
    And to all other ladies, I make moan:
    Pray for my soul, and yield me burial.
    Pray for my soul thou too, Sir Lancelot,
    As thou art a knight peerless."

The voyage of Elaine to Camelot was a favorite subject among artists of the late nineteenth and early twentieth centuries. Doré's engraving shows the scene with all the romantic details dear to the popular imagination of his time. On the dark and wooded shore rise the towers of a castle in the Victorian Gothic style. And though the time is not specified in the poem, the artist shows moonlight glancing upon the rippling waters and castle turrets, intensifying dramatically the whiteness of Elaine in contrast to the black barge, black oarsman, and black shore.

63

The Holy Grail. Detail of a XV century manuscript illumination from a French prose romance of Lancelot. In the Bibliothèque Nationale, Paris, Fr. 120, fol. 524

THE HOLY GRAIL

The romances of Arthur gave the Middle Ages not only stories of love and adventure but also an enduring religious theme, the quest of the Holy Grail. This story did not always belong to the cycle of Arthur, nor was it always Christian. It grew from two very different traditions—Celtic legends of a magic platter which gave food and drink to the brave, and the story, told in the New Testament and expanded in the apocryphal gospels, of the cup or dish which was used at the Last Supper. Early romancers differed widely as to what the Grail was, but in the thirteenth century it was generally accepted as a vessel used at the Last Supper. Joseph of Arimathea, tradition said, filled it with blood from the side of Christ at the Crucifixion and brought it to Britain when he came to Christianize that land. Mediaeval artists represented it as the chalice, familiar to them in the mass, although the word *graal* means a rather deep platter. In the miniature above, this golden chalice, veiled in filmy white, is supported by golden angels and sheds about it a supernatural light, suggested by gold lines.

As times grew more evil, the sacred vessel was hidden from all but a few. Men's desire to find it is the theme of the romances of the quest. In these romances the hero's identity changed with the nature of the Grail he was to win. Perceval was the hero in the oldest remaining Grail romance, Chrétien de Troyes's *Perceval,* or *Conte del Graal,* written about 1175—but Chrétien does not say what the Grail was. Perceval, too, was the hero of Wolfram von Eschenbach's great German poem *Parzival,* written early in the thirteenth century, in which the Grail is a magic stone from heaven. Perceval was married and loved his wife deeply; in Wolfram's poem they lived happily at the Grail castle with their children and were not entirely separated from the world.

Such a hero as Perceval did not harmonize with the mediaeval monastic ideal of the guardian of a holy relic, who should completely renounce all worldly ties. So a new Grail knight, Galahad, was created for this purpose as Lancelot had been created to satisfy the ideal of courtly love. Galahad was the hero of the thirteenth-century French prose romance on which Malory based his Grail story in the *Morte d'Arthur,* establishing this hero as the Grail knight of English literature. The story of Perceval did not disappear, but though it was told in romances, few examples of it in art exist today.

The romancers made Galahad the son of Lancelot, who was comforted for his own failure to achieve the spiritual quest by the fact that it was won by his son. Galahad's mother, Dame Elaine, was descended from Joseph of Arimathea, and in her father's castle of Carbonek the Grail was sometimes to be seen. The child Galahad, according to some romances, was brought up by nuns, the Christian equivalent of the damsels who reared Lancelot beneath the Lake, and in the course of time he came to Arthur's court. At this point Malory takes up the story in detail.

At the court in Camelot great marvels had appeared. Letters "newly written of gold" over the Siege Perilous announced that this vacant place at the Round Table would soon be filled, and on the river there floated a great stone "of red marble, and therein stuck a fair rich sword." None of the knights could draw it, so they knew that some great event was near. Awaiting this, they covered the Siege Perilous with a silken cloth.

Then "all the doors and windows of the palace shut by themself" and there "came in a good old man, and an ancient, clothed all in white, and there was no knight knew from whence he came. And with him he brought a young knight, both on foot, in red arms, without sword or shield, save a scabbard hanging by his side. And these words he said: Peace be with you, fair lords. Then the old man said unto Arthur: Sir, I bring here a young knight, the which is of king's lineage, and of the kindred of Joseph of Aramathie, whereby the marvels of this court, and of strange realms, shall be fully accomplished. . . . And the old knight said unto the young knight: Sir, follow me. And anon he led him unto the Siege Perilous, where beside sat Sir Launcelot; and the good man lift up the cloth, and found there letters that said thus: This is the siege of Galahad." And when Galahad had sat down in that seat wherein no man had ever sat before without great misfortune, the knights said among themselves: "This is he by whom the Sangreal shall be

te famue qu noteut for fer estuulces. aui   et mon lxfaucel le roi refqueos et liv ittes

achieved." In the manuscript illumination above, the ancient man is leading Galahad into Arthur's hall. The silken cloth is already lifted from the Siege Perilous, and Arthur and Lancelot, one on each side of it, point toward the letters. The inlaid marble floor and seats and the banded embroidery of the tablecloth recall those of Italian palaces. Dogs wait beside the table to catch discarded bones, and pages are busy serving, seeming not to notice the unaccustomed happenings.

When the meal was over, the king and his knights "went down from the palace to shew Galahad the adventures of the stone. . . . And anon he laid his hand on the sword, and lightly drew it out of the stone." After this, Arthur held a tournament in which Galahad won over all the knights except Lancelot and Perceval, though he bore no shield because he was waiting for one that God would send him.

Galahad comes to the Round Table. Manuscript illumination, North Italian, about 1380-1400, from a French prose romance of the Grail Quest. In the Bibliothèque Nationale, Paris, Fr. 343, fol. 3

After evensong that day, as the knights sat at the Round Table, suddenly "there entered into the hall the Holy Greal covered with white samite, but there was none might see it, nor who bare it." When it had departed, Sir Gawain led the knights in a vow to seek it for "a twelvemonth and a day, or more if need be," until they had "seen it more openly than it hath been seen here." But Arthur said: "Alas, . . . Sir Gawaine, ye have nigh slain me with the avow and promise that ye have made; for through you ye have bereft me the fairest fellowship and the truest of knighthood that ever were seen together in any realm of the world; for when

The knights take the oath to seek the Grail. Manuscript illumination, North Italian, about 1380–1400, from a French prose romance of the Grail Quest. Bibliothèque Nationale, Paris, Fr. 343, fol. 7

plius qe li uentm air trop a eu uij me   repart cruoi . mes plius qe ge uoi qe
feir honuent si me retonere .

The departure of the knights to seek the Grail. Manuscript illumination, North Italian, about 1380-1400, from a French prose romance of the Grail Quest. In the Bibliothèque Nationale, Paris, Fr. 343, fol. 8

---

hey depart from hence I am sure they all shall never
meet more in this world, for they shall die many in the
quest." But Lancelot answered him: "Comfort yourself; for it shall be unto us a great honour and much
more than if we died in any other places, for of death
we be siccar."

The manuscript page which shows the knights swear-
ing the oath to seek the Grail suggests, with exquisitely
decorative effect, such a scene as might have taken place
in a mediaeval church on the eve of a battle or some other
great adventure. A priest holds the sacred book upon
which Galahad places his hands to take the oath; behind
him the other knights wait their turn, while Arthur
stands at the side. This scene is from a French prose romance of the Grail Quest, written and illuminated in
North Italy. In Malory's romance the knights take the
oath at the Round Table itself after the Grail has vanished, and do not gather at the church until the next
day, when they are ready to depart.

After the service the knights "put on their helms and
departed." As they "rode through the streets of Camelot
. . . there was weeping of the rich and poor, and the
king turned away and might not speak for weeping."
As for the ladies of the court, "they had such sorrow
and heaviness that there might no tongue tell it, for those
knights had held them in honour and charity." In the

miniature of the departure above, the king and his court
wear the costumes fashionable throughout Europe at
the end of the fourteenth century. The tearful Guenevere, in her clinging, boldly patterned gown, is an ap-
pealing figure of delicate and slender grace. The knights'
helmets are crowned with elaborate crests; Galahad's
is a winged cherub symbolizing the guardian angels of
the Grail. The large scale of the figures and the bold,
free style suggest wall painting rather than the elaborate
and detailed technique of most manuscript illuminations.
The animals resemble those of the North Italian painter
Pisanello, who worked about this time.

The knights soon scattered and went their separate
ways to seek the Grail. Galahad had not long to wait
to find his shield; it had hung for centuries behind an
altar in an abbey. This shield was "as white as any snow,
but in the middes was a red cross" which had been made
by the son of Joseph of Arimathea with his own blood.
Fully armed, Galahad was now ready to ride upon the
quest, but he heard "a voice that said: Go thou now,

half." Lancelot sought long and earnestly, though again and again he was warned in visions or by holy men that because of his love for Guenevere he could no more see the Grail unveiled "than a blind man should see a bright sword." Finally he came to the door of a chamber where the Grail was and prayed: "Show me something of that I seek." The door opened and he had a glimpse of "the holy vessel, covered with red samite, and many angels about it," but when he tried to enter, in spite of a voice that forbade him, a breath like fire smote him "and therewith he fell to the earth, and had no power to arise . . . and lost the power of his body, and his hearing, and his seeing. Then felt he many hands about him, which took him up and bare him out of the chamber door, without any amending of his swoon, and left him there, seeming dead to all people. So upon the morrow when it was fair day" the people of the castle found him and tended him. Four and twenty days he lay in a swoon, and when he awoke he knew beyond doubt that he would never see the Grail more closely. So he departed and came to an abbey, "and on the morn he turned unto Camelot, where he found King Arthur and the queen."

thou adventurous knight, to the Castle of the Maidens, and there do thou away the wicked customs."

At this castle seven brothers, strong knights who symbolized the seven deadly sins, held imprisoned a duke's daughters and their ladies. All seven attacked Galahad together, but he overthrew them. Then there came "an old man clothed in religious clothing, and said: Sir, have here the keys of this castle." So Galahad opened the gates and set free the maidens, and when he had summoned the knights of the countryside, whose duty it was to defend the damsels, and made them swear their loyalty, he set forth again upon the quest.

The "old man clothed in religious clothing," with a great key in one hand, is carved on the same ivory casket which shows Tristan and Iseult and Lancelot on the Sword Bridge. In this scene, Galahad, in chain armor with a long surcoat, puts out his hand to receive the key; the seven knights are nowhere to be seen. The carving beside it has no relation to the Grail story, but tells the tale of an old knight who rescued an ungrateful lady from a hairy wild man of the woods. In the Italian miniature opposite, most of the space is filled by the combat before the Castle of the Maidens. Galahad, with the red cross upon both shield and surcoat, has overthrown four of the knights, and of the three still attacking him one already reels from a blow of the hero's lance. At the side stand the old man with the key and the rescued maidens. This miniature, from the same manuscript as the last three, also suggests by its free, bold style the Italian wall paintings of the time.

The adventures of the knights upon the quest were many and often tedious. Gawain, who had led them in taking the vow, spent his time in deeds which had little to do with the Grail, and so, indeed, did most of the fellowship. As Arthur had foreseen, "many of the knights of the Round Table were slain and destroyed, more than

After long wanderings Sir Perceval and Sir Bors met Galahad and together they came to the castle of Carbonek, where Galahad's grandfather, King Pelles, still lived. At this castle the son of Joseph of Arimathea appeared to them, and then came a vision of Christ himself, who showed them the Grail, though not so openly as they were to see it later, "in the city of Sarras in the spiritual place."

Galahad, Perceval, and Bors set sail in a magic ship which King Solomon had made of wood grown from a branch of the Tree of Knowledge brought by Eve out of Eden. In this ship was the Grail, still covered with red samite. The ship bore them to the city of Sarras, in no known land, and there the Grail nourished them for a year while the king of the city kept them in prison. Then the king died and the people chose Galahad to rule them. For a year he was their king, and then at the year's end Joseph of Arimathea himself appeared to him, bearing the Grail, and said: "Come forth the servant of Jesu Christ, and thou shalt see that thou hast much desired to see. And then he began to tremble right hard when the deadly flesh began to behold the spiritual things. Then he held up his hands toward heaven and

said: Lord, I thank thee, for now I see that that hath been
my desire many a day. Now, blessed Lord, would I not
longer live, if it might please thee, Lord. . . . And when
he had said these words Galahad went to Percivale and
kissed him, and commended him to God; and so he went
to Sir Bors and kissed him, and commended him to God,
and said: Fair lord, salute me to my lord, Sir Launcelot,
my father. . . . And therewith he kneeled down . . . and
made his prayers, and then suddenly his soul departed
to Jesu Christ, and a great multitude of angels bare his
soul up to heaven, that the two fellows might well behold it. Also the two fellows saw come from heaven an
hand, but they saw not the body. And then it came right
to the Vessel, and took it . . . and so bare it up to heaven.
Sithen was there never man so hardy to say that he had
seen the Sangreal."

When Galahad was dead, Perceval entered a hermitage and Bors stayed with him for two years. Then
Perceval died too, and Sir Bors buried him and returned
from Sarras to the Round Table to take up his duties in
the world again. And he told the king and the knights

*Galahad overcomes the seven knights and receives the
key of the Castle of the Maidens. Manuscript illumination, North Italian, about 1380-1400, from a French
prose romance of the Grail Quest. In the Bibliothèque
Nationale, Paris, Fr. 343, fol. 15*

there "of the adventures of the Sangreal, such as had
befallen him and his three fellows. . . . And anon Sir Bors
said to Sir Launcelot: Galahad, your own son, saluted
you by me, and after you King Arthur and all the Court.
. . . Then Launcelot took Sir Bors in his arms, and said:
Gentle cousin, ye are right welcome to me, and all that
ever I may do for you and for yours . . . and that I promise you faithfully, and never to fail. And wit ye well,
gentle cousin, Sir Bors, that ye and I will never depart
in sunder whilst our lives may last. Sir, said he, I will as
ye will." "Thus," says Malory, "endeth the story of the
Sangreal, that was briefly drawn out of French into
English, the which is a story chronicled for one of the
truest and the holiest that is in this world."

69

LEFT: *Sir Galahad at a shrine. Illustration by Dante Gabriel Rossetti for an edition of Tennyson's poems published by Edward Moxon, London, 1857. Slightly enlarged*

RIGHT: *The Quest of the Grail. Water color by Elizabeth Siddal (Mrs. Dante Gabriel Rossetti). Severn collection, England*

The quest of the Grail inspired many works of art in the nineteenth century, as was natural in a time of spiritual hunger. Sir Galahad, of course, was the hero of the quest in the English versions. Rossetti's woodcut, above, illustrates a stanza in Tennyson's short poem *Sir Galahad*, first published in 1842:

> When down the stormy crescent goes,
> A light before me swims,
> Between dark stems the forest glows,
> I hear a noise of hymns.
> Then by some secret shrine I ride;
> I hear a voice, but none are there;
> The stalls are void, the doors are wide,
> The tapers burning fair.
> Fair gleams the snowy altar-cloth,
> The silver vessels sparkle clean,
> The shrill bell rings, the censer swings,
> And solemn chaunts resound between.

These lines recall a sentence from Malory: "Then Sir Galahad came unto a mountain where he found an old chapel, and found there nobody, for all, all was desolate; and there he kneeled tofore the altar, and besought God of wholesome counsel." In the woodcut a supernatural light outlines the faces of the ministrants, who, unseen by Galahad, ring the chapel bell. Rossetti later painted a water color from this design.

In the water color by Elizabeth Siddal, Galahad kneels in one of the mysterious boats described in romances of the Grail and in Tennyson's lines:

> Sometimes on lonely mountain-meres
> I find a magic bark.
> I leap on board; no helmsman steers;
> I float till all is dark.
> A gentle sound, an awful light!
> Three angels bear the Holy Grail;
> With folded feet, in stoles of white,
> On sleeping wings they sail.

Miss Siddal had been Rossetti's model and pupil for some years before she married him in 1860. Although her work shows his influence, her figures have an austerity and an air of grave remoteness entirely her own.

The Quest of the Grail was the theme of one of the most notable sets of tapestry produced by the Pre-Raphaelite artists. Burne-Jones began the designs in 1890 and William Morris carried out the weaving at the Merton Abbey works. The first piece was not completed until 1894. The tapestries present the quest as a symbol of the search for religious truth, and though the scenes are based on Malory, they are so freely interpreted and generalized that their meaning is clear without detailed knowledge of the story. The original set was made for W. K. D'Arcy of Stanmore Hall; a duplicate set was woven a little later for his partner, George McCullough, and several pieces were repeated for other clients. The first set later passed into the collection of the Duke of

Westminster, the second into that of Lord Lee of Fareham.

The subjects of the tapestries are: Arthur's Round Table, when the letters appear over the Siege Perilous; the arming and departure of the knights; the failure of Gawain and Ywain; the failure of Lancelot; Galahad's achievement of the Grail; and the ship which bore the knights to Sarras. The arming and departure of the knights, above, recalls Malory's scene of farewell, when the knights "put on their helms and departed, and recommended them all wholly unto the queen; and there was weeping and great sorrow." Guenevere, in the gateway, stands a little apart, saying farewell to Lancelot. Her ladies, in flowing, richly patterned robes, give arms and helms and shields to the knights who "had held them in honour and charity."

Lancelot's failure to win the Grail, a favorite subject in the romances, appealed with equal strength to nineteenth-century artists and poets. In 1857 Rossetti gathered a group of friends, including Burne-Jones and William Morris, to co-operate in decorating the debating hall of the Oxford Union with scenes selected from Malory. Rossetti took as his subjects the failure of Sir Lancelot, and Galahad, Bors, and Perceval beholding the Grail. Burne-Jones chose Merlin and Nimue, and

Morris, Sir Palamedes watching Tristan and Iseult. They began to work that year, but though they had planned to finish in a short time, the project was abandoned incomplete in 1858. The young artists knew nothing of the technique of fresco painting, with its carefully prepared surface and exact timing, and they applied their colors directly on the new brick walls covered only with a layer of whitewash. Before the first painting was finished it had begun to fade. Many of the scenes were never completed, and those which were finished are now only dim ghosts upon the walls. Fortunately a copy had been made of Rossetti's Failure of Sir Lancelot, and Rossetti himself left many sketches for it.

In the Oxford fresco Lancelot lies asleep at the right, his shield hanging upon a tree above him. At the left are a group of singers and a damsel bearing the Grail. Between Lancelot and the Grail stands the vision of Guenevere. Rossetti described the scene in a letter to his American friend Charles Eliot Norton in 1858: "My own subject (for each of us has as yet done only one) is

Guenevere. Study by Dante Gabriel Rossetti for his painting of The Failure of Sir Lancelot, in the Oxford Union, 1857-1858. Birmingham Museum and Art Gallery, England

Sir Launcelot prevented by his sin from entering the Chapel of the San Grail. He has fallen asleep before the shrine full of angels, and between him and it rises in his dream the image of Queen Guenevere, the cause of all. She stands gazing at him with her arms extended in the branches of an apple-tree." The painting was based on Malory's description of Lancelot's first failure on the quest. Lancelot, "half waking and sleeping," lay near a little chapel, his shield hung upon a tree. There he saw a sick knight upon a litter, to whom unseen hands brought the Grail. The holy vessel healed the knight and vanished, and Lancelot, because of his sin, was powerless to awake and follow it. Rossetti discarded the mystic vision of the sick knight and substituted Guenevere as "the cause of all." There is no vision of Guenevere in Malory, but there is a continual sense of her presence in Lancelot's mind, and he confesses to a hermit: "Never did I battle all only for God's sake, but for to win worship and to cause me to be the better beloved." Rossetti expressed the allegorical meaning of the story by showing the queen forever between Lancelot and the Grail. The apple tree and the apple in her hand also suggest Guenevere as another Eve, offering the fruit of the Tree of Knowledge. The drawing above is the figure of

Guenevere from one of Rossetti's studies for this painting.

Swinburne's early poem *Lancelot* must have been influenced by Rossetti's painting, for the poet watched the artist at work in the Oxford Union. In this poem written in 1857 or 1858, but not discovered until 1918, Lancelot dreams that he sees a damsel bearing the Grail. As he looks toward it, the maiden changes into a vision of Guenevere:

> Lo, between me and the light
> Grows a shadow on my sight,
> A soft shade to left and right,
>   Branchèd as a tree.
> Green the leaves that stir between
> And the buds are lithe and green,
> And against it seems to lean
> One in stature as the Queen
>   That I prayed to see.
>
> . . . .
>
> Is it her own face I see
> Thro' the smooth leaves of the tree,
>   Sad and very fair?
> All the wonder that I see
> Fades and flutters over me
> Till I know not what things be
>   As I seemed to know.
> But I see so fair she is,
> I repent me not in this;
> And to kiss her but one kiss
> I would count it for my bliss
>   To be troubled so.
> For she leans against it straight,
> Leans against it all her weight,
> All her shapeliness and state;
> And the apples golden-great
>   Shine about her there.

Burne-Jones's tapestry gives a different interpretation of the failure of Lancelot. Like Rossetti, he omitted the story of the sick knight, but instead of the vision of Guenevere he showed an angel barring the chapel door —a device closer to Malory's descriptions than Rossetti's vision of the queen. The setting in the tapestry is close, also, to Malory's description of the scene preceding the healing of the sick knight. Lancelot "came to a stony cross which departed two ways in waste land; and by the cross was a stone that was of marble, but it was so dark that Sir Launcelot might not wit what it was. Then Sir Launcelot looked by him, and saw an old chapel, and there he weened to have found people; and Sir Launcelot tied his horse till a tree, and there he did off his shield and hung it upon a tree. And then he went to the chapel door, and found it waste and broken. And within he found a fair altar, full richly arrayed with cloth of clene silk, and there stood a fair clean candlestick, which bare six great candles, and the candlestick was of silver. And when Sir Launcelot saw this light he had great will for to enter into the chapel, but he could find no place where he might enter; then was he passing heavy and dismayed. Then he returned and came to his

horse and did off his saddle and bridle, . . . and unlaced his helm, and ungirt his sword, and laid him down to sleep."

Tennyson's description of the failure of Lancelot, in the idyll of *The Holy Grail,* was based on Malory's story of the knight's last glimpse of the Grail. In the poem Lancelot tells the king of the chapel, of his attempt to enter, and of the fiery blast that smote him as a consequence of his rashness:

> "at the last I reach'd a door,
> A light was in the crannies, and I heard,
> 'Glory and joy and honor to our Lord
> And to the Holy Vessel of the Grail!'
> Then in my madness I essay'd the door;
> It gave, and thro' a stormy glare, a heat
> As from a seven-times-heated furnace, I,
> Blasted and burnt, and blinded as I was,
> With such a fierceness that I swoon'd away—
> O, yet methought I saw the Holy Grail,
> All pall'd in crimson samite, and around

The Failure of Sir Lancelot. Tapestry designed by Edward Burne-Jones and woven at William Morris's Merton Abbey Works, 1890-1894. In the collection of the Duke of Westminster

> Great angels, awful shapes, and wings and eyes!
> And but for all my madness and my sin,
> And then my swooning, I had sworn I saw
> That which I saw; but what I saw was veil'd
> And cover'd, and this quest was not for me."

No nineteenth-century pictures of the Grail quest are better known than George Frederic Watts's Sir Galahad and the Grail series painted for the Boston Public Library by the American artist Edwin Austin Abbey. Watts, though a contemporary of the Pre-Raphaelites, did not belong to their group. He was, however, as insistent as they that painting should deal with heroic subjects.

The first version of Watts's *Sir Galahad,* now in the

Sir Galahad. Painting by George Frederic Watts, 1862. In the Fogg Museum of Art, Harvard University

Fogg Museum, was done in 1862. Later, in response to the enthusiasm it aroused, Watts painted another version which he presented to Eton in 1897. While planning the Eton picture he wrote characteristically: "I recognize that from several points of view art would be a most valuable auxiliary in teaching, and nowhere can lessons that may help to form the character of the youth of England be more important than in the great schools where statesmen, and soldiers, and leaders of thought receive their first impressions."

Watts's picture has long been closely associated with Tennyson's poem *Sir Galahad*, published twenty years earlier. When the painting was first exhibited at the Royal Academy in London in 1862, no reference to the poem appeared in the catalogue, though exhibition catalogues of the time were filled with quotations and literary explanations. Nor was there any reference to Tennyson in the catalogue, prepared in consultation with Watts, of the exhibition of the artist's work held in 1897. However, when the picture had been exhibited in 1887, in the schoolrooms adjoining Saint Jude's Church, Whitechapel, the catalogue description of Sir Galahad had closed with the first four lines of Tennyson's poem:

> My good blade carves the casques of men,
> My tough lance thrusteth sure,
> My strength is as the strength of ten,
> Because my heart is pure.

Whether or not the picture was inspired by this poem, the widespread association of the two followed a sound instinct, for in spirit they are closely akin. Watts shared the general enthusiasm for Tennyson and was also his friend, and it seems unlikely that he could have painted the subject without thinking of Tennyson's poem, so long familiar.

Abbey's paintings of the Grail legend combine scenes from the stories of Galahad and Perceval, using Galahad as the hero. The artist was given the commission for the paintings in 1890 and installed the first pictures in the Boston Library in 1895. The series was not finished, however, until 1901. Abbey's first idea for the work was a combination of themes suggesting the literature of many lands. He wrote to a friend shortly after he had received the commission: "As to subject, the great difficulty of generalising the literature of the civilised world is really staggering." The plan he outlined in the letter included something from Chaucer or Shakespeare, to represent England; The Song of Roland, Rabelais, Molière, or Froissart for France; Don Quixote or The Cid for Spain; Dante or Boccaccio for Italy; Homer for Greece; Goethe or a Rhine legend for Germany; a saga for the Scandinavian countries; and Hawthorne for the United States. There was no mention of the Grail story, but within a short time he had decided upon it as international enough to represent all countries.

His choice may have been influenced by the Burne-Jones tapestries. The summer after he received the commission for the Boston paintings Abbey went to England, where he saw much of William Morris at the time when the plans for the Grail tapestries were under way. There is no proof that the Englishman suggested the subject, but it seems likely that the two artists would discuss the work in which they were engaged and that the idea may have come to Abbey in this way.

In the finished series of the Grail in Boston there are fifteen panels, each eight feet high but varying greatly in length, which form a frieze around the room just below the ceiling. Each panel is a separate painting in oil on canvas, fastened to the wall over a coat of white

Galahad receives the key of the Castle of the Maidens. Painting by Edwin Austin Abbey, 1890-1901. In the Boston Public Library

lead. Abbey wrote of his scheme: "My idea is to treat the frieze not precisely in what is known as decorative fashion but to represent a series of paintings, in which the action takes place in a sort of procession (for lack of a better word) in the foreground. The background is there all the same but I try to keep it without incidental interest. Galahad's figure, in scarlet, is the brilliant recurring note, all the way round the room." The artist chose the costumes and architecture of the twelfth century as the most fitting for his paintings, since this was the century in which the first romances were written. He studied the architecture of the period and had a large wardrobe of costumes and armor for his models in the English studio where the paintings were done. But although details were worked out carefully, there is no suggestion of mediaeval feeling in the pictures themselves.

The series begins with the childhood of Galahad and ends with his final vision of the Grail. There is no place in the American painter's scheme for the failure of Lancelot, so often told by mediaeval romances and by nineteenth-century English poets and artists. The picture above, the eighth in the series, shows the same scene that appears on the French ivory casket and in the fourteenth-century Italian manuscript—the "old man in religious clothing" giving Galahad the key of the Castle of the Maidens after he has overcome the evil knights.

Wagner's opera *Parsifal* tells the story of the Grail hero of Chrétien de Troyes and Wolfram von Eschenbach—the French Perceval or German Parzival. The composer wrote the libretto in 1871, two years after Tennyson had retold the story of Galahad at length in English in his idyll *The Holy Grail*. The music was composed in 1878 and 1879, and the opera was first performed at Bayreuth in 1882. It received quick attention from artists interested in the Grail story as well as from lovers of music. Burne-Jones wrote in 1884: "I heard Wagner's Parsifal the other day. . . . He made sounds that are really and truly (I assure you, and I ought to know) the very sounds that were to be heard in the San Graal chapel."

The chief source for the libretto was Wolfram von Eschenbach's *Parzival,* but some details were added from other mediaeval German Grail romances. Wolfram had used French sources, but he gave the legend a new moral significance. According to his poem, Parzival's search for the Grail was not, like Galahad's, for the purpose of finding a personal revelation. It was undertaken to relieve suffering which he himself had prolonged through thoughtless mistakes; it was a symbol of understanding acquired through error, grief, and repentance.

Parzival, according to Wolfram, had been brought up in a forest by his widowed mother, Herzeleide, who wished to keep him in ignorance of the world. But one day he met a group of knights from Arthur's court and admired them so much that he set out to become a knight himself. His mother died of grief after his departure—the first of the unhappy results brought about by his youthful ignorance and selfishness. Soon the hero came upon an ancient prince, and as his mother had told him to respect gray hairs, he willingly took the old man's advice about the ways of the world. From the prince's castle he rode into the realm of the fair queen Kondwiramurs, who was besieged by a mighty king. Parzival overcame him and married the queen. It was no part of Wolfram's idea that his hero should be an ascetic. Indeed, Parzival advised Gawain later: "Friend, in thine hour of strife, let the love of a woman pure and true strengthen thine hand."

Soon Parzival said farewell to his bride and set out to find his mother, for his conscience was beginning to prick him for his thoughtless departure. By accident he came, still an inexperienced youth, to the castle of the Grail. There he beheld many marvels. A wounded king lay upon a couch in a great hall, where lights blazed and many knights surrounded him. A squire entered carrying a bleeding lance, and then came a fair damsel who bore aloft "that thing which men call the Grail." From it a hundred squires took whatever food and drink the knights desired, for the Grail was the source of all the castle's life.

Parzival wondered at these sights, but remembered all too well one part of the old prince's advice—not to ask questions. So he kept silent, and when he woke the next morning the castle was empty. He rode forth, to be met by reproaches because he had not asked a question which would have healed the wounded king. Even at Arthur's court, Kundrie, the Grail messenger, denounced him as dishonored and accursed. Smarting under the sense that his punishment was out of all proportion to his unconscious offense, he resolved to renounce the service of a God who was so unjust. But he was determined to find the Grail castle again and heal the king.

After long wanderings he came at last, on a Good Friday, to a hermit who, men said, might help him in his search for the castle. Through the hermit's teaching

Parzival came to understand that it was not God's injustice but his own lack of wisdom and experience which had thwarted him. A man of more perception and compassion would have thought first of the suffering king and not of his own behavior. And such sad results, though hard, were not unnatural, for much of the world's suffering comes from ignorance rather than from evil intent. From the hermit Parzival learned of other misfortunes he had caused through rashness and ignorance—his mother's death from sorrow and the fact that he had killed, unfairly and without cause, a knight who was his own kin. The hermit told him about the Grail, too, and the wounded king. The Grail was a magic stone from heaven on which appeared, from time to time, the laws which governed its guardians and the names of those called to its service. The king, Anfortas, was Parzival's uncle, who had been wounded because he had transgressed the laws of the Grail by loving unworthily. He had to suffer until the knight destined to heal him and be his successor should come and ask "What aileth thee?" Parzival was this destined knight, but since he had lost his first opportunity he would have to wait until heaven led him again to the castle; he could not find it through his own striving, but only through faith and patient waiting.

Humble and comforted in mind, Parzival returned to Arthur's court, from which he presently set out again on long adventures, among them a visit to the castle of the enchanter Klingsor. At last he came again to the Round Table, where Kundrie appeared once more and told him that the time had now come for her to lead him to the Grail castle. There he asked Anfortas, "What aileth thee, mine uncle?" The king was healed, and Parzival was recognized as the new king and guardian of the Grail. His wife and sons arrived at the castle, where they all lived in happiness and in the service of the Grail. In later years one of these sons, Lohengrin, was among those commanded to go into the world and govern kingless lands.

In making an opera from this complicated story, Wagner had to change and condense his material greatly. The romance was reduced to three acts. In the first act, Parsifal, a "guileless Fool," finds his way to the forest of the Grail castle. As Wagner considered his theme distinctly religious, he explained the Grail as the cup of the Last Supper rather than as a magic stone. The hero is led into the presence of the wounded king, Amfortas, but as he stands stupidly by and asks no questions, he is thrown out angrily by the Grail attendants. In the second act Wagner symbolized all the experiences by which Parsifal learned wisdom and compassion in one scene of temptation by fair women and one encounter with Klingsor. From the enchanter, Parsifal wrests the spear with which Amfortas has been wounded. Wolfram had never fully explained the bleeding spear, but Wagner followed other legends in calling it the spear which

had pierced the side of Christ upon the Cross. In the third act, Parsifal, after many years, comes once more to the Grail castle on a Good Friday and heals Amfortas. But he heals the king, not by a question which symbolizes compassion, but by touching him with the spear. This change weakens the emphasis which Wolfram—and Wagner in other parts of the opera—placed upon the hero's growth in wisdom.

Other important changes are the complicated nature of Kundry, who, in the opera, is half good, half evil, and the absence of any reference to Arthur and his court. In Wolfram's romance the Round Table and its knights represented the world as contrasted with the service of the Grail. Wagner wished to oppose absolute good with absolute evil instead of mere worldliness, so he used the magician Klingsor as the embodiment of evil. In Wolfram's romance he had been a figure of magic, neither bad nor good. Finally, Parsifal's whole nature is changed in the opera. There is no place in his life for the love of woman, which Wolfram had praised so highly. He is a Galahad under another name.

Wagner left detailed directions for the settings of

The hall of the Grail castle: setting for the first and third acts of Wagner's "Parsifal." Designed by Joseph Urban for the production by the Metropolitan Opera in 1919

his operas, for he considered words, music, and the picture on the stage as essential parts of one great whole. Joseph Urban's drawing for the hall of the Grail castle, made for the Metropolitan Opera's production of *Parsifal* in 1919, suggests both the dignity of the legend and Wagner's stately music. In this hall the knights of the Grail assemble in the first and last acts of the opera, summoned by the pealing of bells. Beneath the great dome a semicircular table is ready for them, and behind it is the raised couch of the wounded king, whose bearded head is faintly visible at the right. Before the couch the Grail rests, veiled, upon an altar. At the end of the opera Parsifal uncovers it and it glows red as blood. A flood of light pours upon it from the dome and a white dove descends in token of God's favor, while the music dies slowly away with the sound of voices so soft that they might come from some far, spiritual land.

ROMANCERS AND CHRONICLERS
MENTIONED IN THE TEXT

BÉROUL, French. French verse romance of Tristan, about 1190.

CHRÉTIEN DE TROYES, French. French verse romances: Lancelot (The Knight of the Cart), about 1170; Perceval (Conte del Graal), about 1175.

GEOFFREY OF MONMOUTH, Welsh. Latin pseudo-chronicle, *Historia Regum Brittaniae,* "History of the Kings of Britain," between 1136 and 1138.

GOTTFRIED VON STRASSBURG, German. German verse romance of Tristan, about 1210.

LAYAMON, English. Chronicle, or Brut, named from Brutus, mythical ancestor of the Britons, first story of Arthur in English, between 1175 and 1205.

SIR THOMAS MALORY, English. English prose romance, the *Morte d'Arthur,* completed 1469.

NENNIUS, Welsh. Latin chronicle, the *Historia Britonum,* containing first known record of Arthur, about 826.

THOMAS OF BRITAIN, Anglo-Norman. French verse romance of Tristan, about 1185.

WACE, Anglo-Norman. French verse chronicle, *Roman de Brut,* based on Geoffrey of Monmouth's *Historia,* 1155.

WILLIAM OF MALMESBURY, English. Latin chronicle, *De Gestis Regum Angolorum,* "Concerning the Deeds of the English Kings," 1125.

WOLFRAM VON ESCHENBACH, German. German verse romance of Parzival, about 1205.

ARTISTS MENTIONED IN THE TEXT

EDWIN AUSTIN ABBEY, American painter and illustrator, 1852-1911.

ADOLPHE APPIA, Swiss stage designer and critic, 1862-1928.

AUBREY BEARDSLEY, English illustrator, 1872-1898.

EDWARD BURNE-JONES, English painter and designer, 1833-1898.

CHARLES J. CONNICK, American designer and worker in stained glass, contemporary.

GUSTAVE DORÉ, French illustrator and painter, 1832-1883.

EDMUND DULAC, illustrator and painter, born in France, naturalized in England, 1882-.

HAROLD R. FOSTER, cartoonist and painter, born in Halifax, Nova Scotia, contemporary

HOLMAN HUNT, English painter and illustrator, 1827-1910.

DANIEL MACLISE, British illustrator, 1811-1870.

JOHN EVERETT MILLAIS, English painter and illustrator, 1829-1896.

WILLIAM MORRIS, English craftsman, designer, painter, and author, 1834-1896.

HOWARD PYLE, American illustrator, painter, and author, 1853-1911.

ARTHUR RACKHAM, English illustrator and painter, 1867-1939.

DANTE GABRIEL ROSSETTI, English painter, illustrator, and poet, 1828-1882.

ELIZABETH ELEANOR SIDDAL (Mrs. Dante Gabriel Rossetti), English, about 1834-1862.

JOSEPH URBAN, stage designer and decorator, born in Austria, naturalized in America, 1872-1933.

GEORGE FREDERIC WATTS, English painter, 1817-1904.

None of the early artists who painted Arthurian stories are known by name except Jörg Kölderer, Friedrich Lebenbacher, and Max Reichlich, the three Germans who restored the frescoes of Castle Runkelstein by order of Maximilian I between 1503 and 1511.

BOOKS SUGGESTED FOR FURTHER READING

ROMANCES

Chrétien de Troyes. *Arthurian Romances by Chrétien de Troyes,* translated by W. W. Comfort (Everyman's Library). New York, 1914. Erec and Enide, Cliges, Yvain, and Lancelot (The Knight of the Cart). Quotations in the text are from this edition.

Geoffrey of Monmouth. *History of the Kings of Britain* (Everyman's Library). New York, no date. Quotations in the text are from this edition.

Gottfried von Strassburg. *The Story of Tristan and Iseult,* translated by Jessie L. Weston. London, 1907. An abridged prose translation with additions from two of Gottfried's continuators. Quotations in the text are from this edition.

The High History of the Holy Grail, translated by Sebastian Evans (Everyman's Library). New York, no date. The early French prose romance of Perlesvaux, a Perceval form of the Grail story.

Layamon. *Arthurian Chronicles Represented by Wace and Layamon* (Everyman's Library). New York, 1928. The Arthurian portions of Layamon's chronicle. Quotations in the text are from this edition.

Sir Thomas Malory. *Le Morte d'Arthur* (Everyman's Library). New York, 1934. 2 vols. Quotations in the text are from this edition.

Merlin, or The Early History of King Arthur. Early English Text Society, London, 1899. 2 vols. Original Series, vol. I is no. 10, 112; vol. II is no. 21, 36. A translation, about 1450-1460, of a French prose romance.

Le Morte Arthure (The Riverside Literature Series). Boston [1912]. A fourteenth-century English metrical romance, closely resembling the source used by Malory in his last books.

W. Newell. *King Arthur and the Table Round.* Boston, 1897. A prose paraphrase of parts of Chrétien de Troyes's Perceval.

Il Novellino: The Hundred Old Tales. Translated from the Italian by Edward Storer. London and New York [1925]. A late thirteenth-century prose compilation containing stories of Tristan and Iseult and Lancelot and the Damsel of Scalot.

Sir Lancelot of the Lake: A French Prose Romance of the Thirteenth Century. Translated from a MS in the Bibliothèque Nationale (Fonds français, 344) with an introduction and notes by Lucy Allen Paton. London and New York, 1929. Quotations from the prose Lancelot in the text are from this edition.

H. O. Sommer. *Vulgate Version of the Arthurian Romances,* Washington, 1909-1916. 7 vols. Authoritative edition of the Old French prose texts, with narrative marginal notes in English.

Thomas of Britain. *The Romance of Tristram and Ysolt,* by Thomas of Britain, translated from the Old French and the Old Norse by Roger Sherman Loomis. New York, revised edition, 1931.

Wace. *Arthurian Chronicles Represented by Wace and Layamon* (Everyman's Library). New York, 1928. Quotations in the text are from this edition or its introduction.

Wolfram von Eschenbach. *The Story of Parzival and the Grail,* interpreted and discussed by Margaret E. Richey. Oxford, 1935. A partial translation, with synopses of omitted portions.

HISTORICAL AND CRITICAL WORKS

Paolo d'Ancona, "Gli Affreschi del Castello di Manta," *L'Arte,* vol. VIII, 1905, pp. 94-106 and 183-198. Discusses the frescoes at the castle of La Manta. Francesco Novati corrects the identification of one of the Nine Worthy Ladies in *Rassegna d'arte,* vol. XI, 1911, p. 63, n. 18.

T. Ashcroft. *English Art and English Society.* London [1936]. Note especially pages 106-185, on the nineteenth century.

R. F. Brinkley. *Arthurian Legends in the Seventeenth Century.* Johns Hopkins Monographs in Literary History, no. III. Göttingen and Baltimore, 1932.

J. D. Bruce. *Evolution of Arthurian Romance from the Beginnings to the Year 1300.* Baltimore, 1923. 2 vols. Valuable summaries and bibliographies of romances.

G(eorgiana) B(urne)-J(ones). *Memorials of Edward Burne-Jones.* London, 1904. 2 vols.

D. L. Chambers. "Tennysoniana: The Lady of Shalott," *Modern Language Notes,* vol. XVIII, Dec., 1903, pp. 227-228. Discusses the sources of *The Lady of Shalott.*

R. C. Clephan. *The Tournament.* London, 1919, chaps. I-III. Discussion of tournaments in general and Arthurian Round Tables.

R. G. Collingwood. *Roman Britain and the English Settlements.* Oxford, 1937. Book IV, chap. XIX, "Britain in the Fifth Century."

Ettore Gabricci and Ezio Levi. *Lo Steri di Palermo.* Milan, no date. The fullest treatment of the paintings of the Chiaramonte Palace at Palermo. Thoroughly illustrated.

E. GARDNER. *The Arthurian Legend in Italian Literature.* New York, 1930.

LAURA HIBBARD LOOMIS. "The Table of the Last Supper in Religious and Secular Iconography," *Art Studies,* vol. V, 1927, pp. 71-88. Discusses the relationship between the Table of the Last Supper and the Round Table.

ROGER S. LOOMIS. *Arthurian Legends in Mediaeval Art.* Part 2 in collaboration with Laura Hibbard Loomis. London and New York, 1938. The most authoritative and fully illustrated work on this subject.

ROGER S. LOOMIS. "Chivalric and Dramatic Imitations of Arthurian Romance," *Mediaeval Studies in Memory of A. Kingsley Porter.* Cambridge (Mass.), 1939. An invaluable collection of references to Arthurian tournaments and Round Tables and their relation to drama.

E. V. LUCAS. *Edwin Austin Abbey.* New York, 1921. 2 vols. For the Holy Grail paintings in Boston, see especially vol. I, pp. 227 to end; vol. II, pp. 280-284 and 359-361.

J. W. MACKAIL. *The Life of William Morris.* London, 1907. 2 vols.

H. C. MARILLIER. *Dante Gabriel Rossetti.* London, 1899. Two later editions.

H. C. MARILLIER. *History of the Merton Abbey Tapestry Works.* London, 1927. Illustrates all the Burne-Jones tapestries of the Holy Grail.

RAIMOND VAN MARLE. *Italian Schools of Painting,* vol. VII. The Hague, 1926. Chapter II includes a description of the paintings at the castle of La Manta. Well illustrated.

G. H. MAYNADIER. *The Arthur of the English Poets.* Boston and New York, 1907. A classic for the period covered.

C. B. MILLICAN. *Spenser and the Table Round.* Harvard Studies in Comparative Literature, vol. VIII. Cambridge (Mass.), 1932.

ANTONIO MORASSI. *Storia della pittura nella Venezia Tridentina.* Rome, 1934. Castle Runkelstein (Roncolo) discussed and illustrated on pp. 295-323.

ERWIN POESCHEL. *Das Burgenbuch von Graubünden.* Zürich, 1930. The Tristan fresco at Castle Rhäzüns is described on pp. 145-146.

EDOUARD SANDOZ. "Tourneys in the Arthurian Tradition," *Speculum, a Journal of Mediaeval Studies,* vol. XIX, no. 4, Oct., 1944. The French text of a tournament book in the Hofer collection at Harvard, with notes on similar manuscripts in the United States which give the traditional arms of the knights of the Round Table.

VIDA D. SCUDDER. *The Morte Darthur of Sir Thomas Malory.* New York, 1917. Special emphasis upon Malory's treatment of character.

IRIS ESTHER SELLS. *Matthew Arnold and France.* Cambridge (Mass.), 1933. See pp. 140 ff. for the sources of Arnold's treatment of the Tristan story.

F. J. SNELL. *King Arthur's Country.* London, 1926. Discusses the identity and traditions of places named in the romances.

H. O. TAYLOR. *The Mediaeval Mind.* New York, 1914. 2 vols. Discusses mediaeval culture. Chapter XXIV deals with romantic chivalry and courtly love, including the romances of Tristan and Lancelot; chapter XXV with Wolfram von Eschenbach's Parzival.

A. TILLEY. *Studies in the French Renaissance.* Cambridge (Eng.), 1922. Chapter II, "The Prose Romances of Chivalry," gives a brief but valuable account of early printed romances.

PIETRO TOESCA. *La Pittura e la miniature nelle Lombardia.* Milan, 1912. Invaluable illustrations of North Italian wall paintings and manuscript illuminations to the middle of the XV century.

GEORGE M. TREVELYAN. *British History in the Nineteenth Century and After (1782-1919).* London and New York [1938].

GEORGE M. TREVELYAN. *English Social History.* London and New York, 1943.

EUGENE VINAVER. *Malory.* Oxford, 1929. A study of Malory's romance and its sources.

R. WITHINGTON. *English Pageantry.* Cambridge (Eng.), 1918. 2 vols. Vol. I, pp. 85-100, gives a general discussion of tournaments and Arthurian Round Tables.

H. E. WROOT. "Pre-Raphaelite Windows at Bradford," *International Studio,* vol. LXIII, pp. 69-73, Nov., 1917. Illustrates and discusses the stained-glass windows of the story of Tristan and Iseult done in 1862 by the firm of Morris, Marshall, Faulkner and Company.

The spelling of Arthurian proper names has varied widely with country, time, and individual preference. The variation is reflected in this book, as the spellings in quotations have not been altered. In the rest of the text the names of the chief characters follow, in general, the forms used in the first version of the story quoted, unless these forms are not commonly known. In the descriptions of Wagner's operas, however, the composer's own spellings have been used because of their familiarity.

Metropolitan Museum of Art
Publications in Reprint

Egyptological Titles

Davies, Norman de Garis
The Tomb of Ken-Amun at Thebes (2 vols. in 1)
  (Metropolitan Museum of Art Egyptian Expedition Publications, Vol. V: 1930)

Davies, Norman de Garis
The Tomb of Nefer-Hotep at Thebes (2 vols. in 1)
  (Metropolitan Museum of Art Egyptian Expedition Publications, Vol. IX: 1933)

Davies, Norman de Garis
The Tomb of Rekh-Mi-Re at Thebes (2 vols. in 1)
  (Metropolitan Museum of Art Egyptian Expedition Publications, Vol. XI: 1943)

Hayes, William C.
The Burial Chamber of theTreasurer Sobk-Mose from Er-Rizeikat
  (Metropolitan Museum of Art Papers, No. 9: 1939)

Hayes, William C.
Glazed Tiles from a Palace of Ramesses II at Kantir
  (Metropolitan Museum of Art Papers, No. 3: 1937)

Hayes, William C.
Ostraka and Name Stones from the Tomb of Sen-Mut (No. 71) at Thebes
  (Metropolitan Museum of Art Egyptian Expedition Publications, Vol. XV: 1942)

Hayes, William C.
The Texts in the Mastabeh of Se'n-Wosret-Ankh at Lisht
  (Metropolitan Museum of Art Egyptian Expedition Publications, Vol. XII: 1937)

Mace, Arthur C. and Winlock, Herbert E.
The Tomb of Senebtisi at Lisht
  (Metropolitan Museum of Art Egyptian Expedition Publications, Vol. I: 1916)

White, Hugh G. Evelyn
The Monasteries of the Wadi 'N Natrun (3 vols.)
  (Metropolitan Museum of Art Egyptian Expedition Publications, Vols. II,
  VII and VIII: 1926-1933)

  New Coptic Texts from the Monastery of Saint Macarius (1926)
  The History of the Monasteries of Nitria and of Scetis, ed. by
    Walter Hauser (1932)
  The Architecture and Archaeology, ed. by Walter Hauser (1933)

Schiller, A. Arthur
Ten Coptic Legal Texts
> (Metropolitan Museum of Art, Dept. of Egyptian Art Publications,
> Vol. II: 1932)

Winlock, Herbert E.
The Temple of Rameses I at Abydos (2 vols. in 1)
> (Metropolitan Museum of Art Papers, No. 1, Pt. 1 and No. 5, 1921-1937)
> > **Bas-Reliefs from the Temple of Rameses I at Abydos** (1921)
> > **The Temple of Ramesses I at Abydos** (1937)

Winlock, Herbert E.
Materials Used at the Embalming of King Tut-Ankh-Amun
> (Metropolitan Museum of Art Papers, No. 10: 1941)

Winlock, H. E.; Crum, W. E.; and White, Hugh G. Evelyn
The Monastery of Epiphanius at Thebes (2 vols.)
> (Metropolitan Museum of Art Egyptian Expedition Publications, Vols.
> III and IV: 1926)
> > **The Archaeological Material,** by H. E. Winlock;
> > **The Literary Material,** by W. E. Crum
> > **Coptic Ostraca and Papyri,** by W. E. Crum;
> > **Greek Ostraca and Papyri,** by H. G. E. White

Winlock, Herbert E.; White, Hugh G. Evelyn; and Oliver, James H.
The Temple of Hibis in El Khargeh Oasis (2 vols. in 1)
> (Metropolitan Museum of Art Egyptian Expedition Publications, Vols. XIII
> and XIV: 1938-1941)
> > **The Excavations,** by H. E. Winlock (1941)
> > **Greek Inscriptions,** by H. G. E. White and James H. Oliver (1938)

Winlock, Herbert E.
The Tomb of Queen Meryet-Amun at Thebes
> (Metropolitan Museum of Art Egyptian Expedition Publications, Vol. VI:
> 1932)

Winlock, Herbert E.
The Treasure of El Lahun
> (Metropolitan Museum of Art, Dept. of Egyptian Art Publications.
> Vol. IV: 1934)

Miscellaneous Titles

Avery, C. Louise
An Exhibition of Early New York Silver (1931)

Clouzot, Henri and Morris, Frances
Painted and Printed Fabrics (1927)

Grancsay, Stephen V.
The Armor of Galiot De Genouilhac
> (Metropolitan Museum of Art Papers, No. 4: 1937)

Grinnell, Isabel Hoopes
Greek Temples (1943)

Halsey, R. T. Haines
Catalogue of an Exhibition of Silver used in New York, New Jersey, and the South (1911)

Howe, Winifred E.
A History of The Metropolitan Museum of Art (1913)

Life in America
> A Special Loan Exhibition of Paintings Held During the Period of the New York World's Fair, April 24 to October 29 (1939)

Metropolitan Museum Studies, Vol. V, Part I (1934)

Myres, John L.
Handbook of The Cesnola Collection of Antiquities from Cyprus (1914)

Priest, Alan
Chinese Sculpture in The Metropolitan Museum of Art (1944)

Priest, Alan
Costumes from the Forbidden City (1945)

Scherer, Margaret R.
About the Round Table: King Arthur in Art and Literature (1945)

The Bulletin of The Metropolitan Museum of Art, 1905-1942
> With Cumulative Index (38 vols.)